SHARING THE PAST

NORTHAMPTONSHIRE BLACK HISTORY

" ...an overview of Northamptonshire's connections to the wider world, and especially to Africa, the Caribbean and the Indian subcontinent... "

Our book introduces you to previously hidden aspects of the past, and to people whose stories may surprise you.

Northamptonshire Black History Association

First published: 2008
Published by Northamptonshire Black History Association
Copyright © Northamptonshire Black History Association 2008

ISBN: 978-0-9557139-1-0

Northamptonshire Black History Association
Doddridge Centre
109 St James Road
Northampton NN5 5LD
Tel: 01604 590967 Email: admin@northants-black-history.org.uk
www.northants-black-history.org.uk

Printed by Eagle Graphics (Printers) Ltd
Unit 1, Firbank Court
Leighton Buzzard LU7 4YJ
Tel: 01525 384893 Email: graphics@egp.uk.com

This book is dedicated to the pioneering

community leaders who have enriched

the lives of Northamptonshire settlers

from the Caribbean, Africa and the

Indian subcontinent and helped to make

Northamptonshire a better place

Sharing the Past: Contents

Contents

Acknowledgements

Sharing the Past: Acknowledgements

This book was written by Ismael Ali, Monica Babb, Terry Bracher, John Brownell, Julia Bush, Ruchira Leisten, Wajiha Mohammad, Austin Madu, Marjorie Morgan, Leticia Narh, Donna Palmer-Smith, Chris Pounds, Anne-Marie Sandos, Nikki Taylor and Victor Ukaegbu. The Finding Out More appendix was written by Julia Bush, Paul Bracey, Jenny Moran, Terry Bracher and Rachel Silverson.

The editors of the book were Terry Bracher, Julia Bush, Ruchira Leisten and Donna Palmer-Smith, assisted by Paul Bingham, Paul Crofts, June Gulley, Linda Hoddle and Marjorie Morgan. Chapters were also checked by Shirley Brownbill, Pat Sinclair, Sally Sokoloff and Morcea Walker. The illustrations were edited by Paul Bingham and Julia Bush, assisted by Angela Ghavami and Nikki Taylor. Members of the Northamptonshire Black History Association Committee offered advice and support throughout the production process. NBHA's HLF-funded education project, Shaping the Future, has developed in parallel with the present book, under the leadership of Nikki Taylor. We are pleased that our book provides useful support to the NBHA curriculum packs and loan boxes produced during 2007-08.

Thanks are due for the research which has made the book possible. First and foremost, we thank all the Northamptonshire people who recorded their life histories through the Northamptonshire Black History Project, 2002-05. This project, funded by the Heritage Lottery Fund, the Home Office and Northamptonshire County Council, was led by Carolyn Abel (director), Julia Drake (oral history) and Nikki Taylor (community research and archives). A large group of sessional workers and volunteers helped to research the Black and Asian presence in Northamptonshire's past, collecting evidence now accessible online through the NBHA database (www.northants-black-history.org.uk). Over the past three years we have continued to expand our knowledge of Northamptonshire's Black History, with the help of NBHA members and supporters. Black History researchers have received excellent support over the years from staff at the Northamptonshire Central Library, the Northamptonshire Record Office and the Northampton Museums Service.

Illustrations are an important part of this book. Paul Bingham played a central role in choosing the illustrations, including many of his own photographs. Other owners and copyright-holders are gratefully acknowledged below, numbers indicating the page location of the relevant picture. We have made efforts to contact all copyright holders, but in a few cases have been unable to establish definite ownership. If any readers have further information, or believe copyright has been wrongly attributed, please contact NBHA and we will make the necessary corrections as soon as possible.

Finally, we wish to acknowledge the financial sponsorship which has enabled us to produce a high-quality, well-illustrated book at an affordable price. The University of Northampton subsidised the costs of publication, as part of its ongoing partnership with the Northamptonshire Black History Association. The Heritage Lottery Fund also contributed, as part of the Shaping the Future education project. Northamptonshire Black History Association itself was the third funder. In 2005 the Northamptonshire Black History Project won the CILIP Libraries Change Lives national award – and a decision was taken to put the prize money towards a Big Book, summarising our research and making it accessible to everyone. Three years later, here it is!

Picture credits

Introduction: Sharing the Past

This book is about sharing the past for the sake of our shared future.

Northamptonshire is a county rich in local history. Every year new books and films appear, new museums open, and new exhibitions are mounted to celebrate local achievements. Many of us love to record the transition of ordinary communities from past to present, and to commemorate people, buildings and customs lost to the onrush of modernity. But how many local historians try to place our county's past in a worldwide context, as well as within a wider picture of British history? We need a better understanding of how Northamptonshire people have interacted with the rest of the world. This interaction has helped to cause recent migration to Britain from the Caribbean, Africa and the Indian subcontinent, as well as being one of its results. Northamptonshire's worldwide links have strengthened since the Second World War, and two-way connections between the county and distant parts of the world can also be traced back through four previous centuries.

Sharing the Past provides exciting proof that "local" history has always been more than just "local". Northamptonshire shares its past, as well as its present and future, with many different places and cultures. The county's wealthy families played their part in the histories of colonisation and of the British slave trade. Northamptonshire families invested in the Caribbean plantations, hired Black servants, and sent their sons to trade, fight and often die in the service of a growing empire.

While rich people left the county in the hope of becoming richer, the Northamptonshire poor found themselves becoming reluctant emigrants as soldiers, sailors and assisted pauper settlers. Meanwhile African and Asian people travelled in the opposite direction. The Black history of the port cities of London, Bristol and Liverpool is gradually becoming better-known, but a lot more research is needed on the stories of early Black visitors and settlers in smaller towns and rural areas like Northamptonshire.

We hope that *Sharing the Past* will encourage other counties to re-examine their local history, in search of unexpected diversity and interesting individuals whose stories bring the history of empire vividly to life. There is a need to put local Black British history firmly on the map, especially in a period when the concept of "Britishness" is being hotly debated by politicians and the media.

Every book has its own history, and this one is no exception. *Sharing the Past* is the outcome of three years of intensive research led by the community-based Northamptonshire Black History Project, funded by the Heritage Lottery Fund from 2002-05. The Project resulted from longer-term local interest in Black British history, and was followed by the foundation of the Northamptonshire Black History Association (NBHA) as a community-based membership organisation committed both to research and to education. NBHA has successfully developed Black History curriculum materials for local schools, as well as running a busy programme of community history.

One of NBHA's most important roles is to continue and complete the task of depositing over two hundred oral history recordings at the Northamptonshire Record Office. Northamptonshire has one of the best oral history archives in the country, and the recorded life histories of first-generation settlers in the county have provided a wealth of evidence to inform the later chapters in this book. As a mark of respect for this generation, our book is dedicated to pioneering local community leaders: your work will never be forgotten.

Sharing the Past aims to interest the widest possible readership, and provides the first continuous narrative linking together all our favourite Black History stories. Happy and sad, famous and infamous – there is something here for everyone. Chapter One takes us back to the first evidence of a Black presence in Northamptonshire, and concludes as the British slave trade was making its mark at the end of the seventeenth century. Chapter Two outlines the development of British rule in India during the eighteenth and nineteenth centuries, describing its impact upon Northamptonshire visitors to India who included poor soldiers and devoted missionaries as well as rich fortune-hunters. Chapters Three and Four examine evidence of Northamptonshire's involvement in the Transatlantic Slave Trade, including its consequences for young Black children brought here as servants, as well as the county's prominent role in the anti-slavery campaign. Victorian Northamptonshire is further explored in the two following chapters, which discuss ordinary people's worldwide links in the nineteenth century and uncover the life stories of some striking overseas visitors to the county.

Moving forward into the twentieth century, Chapter Seven explores the contribution of the British colonies and their peoples to the two World Wars, not forgetting the roles played by Black people settled in Northamptonshire. Chapters Eight, Nine and Ten describe how much larger numbers of people from the countries of the former British Empire have travelled to live in Northamptonshire during the last sixty years. Experiences of hard work, difficult adjustment, and sometimes local hostility were generally alleviated by good humour and a determination to succeed. There was more to life than work. In Chapter Eleven and Chapter Twelve, our focus shifts to the part which Black sportsmen and women, and Black entertainers, have played in Northamptonshire's history. Finally, we turn to the important subjects of community leadership and public service. Black settlers have helped themselves by helping each other. In the process they have made a major contribution to public services in the county, benefitting both Black and White communities and laying foundations for a successfully shared future.

Did you know that Northamptonshire was home to a Saracen crossbow-maker in the thirteenth century? Did you know that parish registers record the baptisms and deaths of named Black individuals, from the sixteenth century onwards? Have you ever come across a Black servant's grave in a country churchyard? Does your knowledge of famous visitors to Northamptonshire include the stories of Susi and Chuma, guides to the African missionary David Livingstone, and of Dadabhai Naoroji, the first Black British Member of Parliament? Supported by the famous "Member for India", Charles Bradlaugh, Naoroji denounced the suffering inflicted by imperial rule at Northampton Guildhall in 1888. With hindsight, we can interpret this event as a warning of the future dismantling of the British Empire. It is very unlikely that the appreciative local audience either expected or wished for such an outcome. Northamptonshire people played a brave role in various imperialist wars during the following decades, before finally accepting the inevitable.

At every turn, Northamptonshire's Black History is full of surprises and unexpected turns. We hope you will enjoy getting to know it better.

The Early Black Presence

Black people have been in Britain since Roman times. Moorish soldiers from North Africa were part of a Roman army during its occupation of Britain. A division of Moors, Numerus Maurorum Aurelianorum, was stationed along Hadrian's Wall near Carlisle, while archaeological evidence highlights a number of Black Africans, not necessarily soldiers, buried in York. The Roman Emperor Septimus Severus, born in Libya, also died in York. There is no conclusive evidence of Moorish soldiers or other Black Africans in Northamptonshire during this period. We can only speculate whether they would have visited Roman settlements such as those at Towcester and Irchester, or travelled along the Roman roads that are still visible in the county, notably Watling Street (now the A5), one of main arteries of communication. To find the first written evidence of a possible Black presence in Northamptonshire, we need to travel forward to the thirteenth century.

Contained in the records of the Court of Chancery, known as Close Rolls, there is a mandate from King John "to the constable of Northampton to retain Peter the Saracen, the maker of crossbows, and another with him, for the King's service, and allow him 9d. a day. Freemantle, 26th July 1205." The word "Saracen" was normally used to describe someone who is of North African or Middle-

Peter the Saracen record, 1205

Eastern origin, as well as people of Islamic faith. We may not know if Peter the Saracen was Black, but this evidence does start to challenge the notion that Black people only arrived in Northamptonshire in the twentieth century.

Peter the Saracen appears to have been in England since 1194, where he is mentioned in financial records called the Pipe Rolls. Little is known about him apart from the obvious fact that he was a skilled craftsman, but it leads us to ask why he was brought to Northampton. How many others like Peter were living in or around the town and indeed the whole of Britain at that time?

By the thirteenth century Northampton had become an important and prosperous regional centre, one of the largest towns in England with a population estimated to be around three thousand. Simon de Senlis, Earl of Northampton, had fortified it in 1089 and a castle was erected in the following century. The footprint of the town walls is still visible today in the shape of the inner ring road, while the railway station now occupies the site of the castle. Northampton was established as a royal court around 1130 and Richard I granted the town its first charter in 1189. By 1205 it was favoured by King John. This was also the time of the Crusades, when Christian armies set out from across Europe to conquer the Holy Land and impose their religion on its Muslim inhabitants. The round Church of the Holy Sepulchre (modelled on the original in Jerusalem) is one of the few lasting monuments to this period of the town's history. Just as Moorish soldiers had been brought from North Africa by the Roman army, so it is possible that people from North Africa or the Middle East accompanied the crusaders back to Britain, bringing specialist skills that were highly valued and in short supply, such as crossbow making.

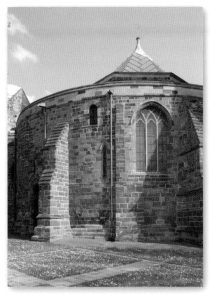

Holy Sepulchre Church, Northampton

Simon de Senlis – crusader

By the time Peter the Saracen arrived in Northampton, the town and its vicinity already had a diverse population. A Jewish community together with a synagogue was recorded in the twelfth century. Elsewhere, there is a reference to Roger le Turk, described as serjeant at Towcester and a witness to the confirmation by Wilbert the porter to Henry de Stotevile of the eleven acres granted to him by Felicia, Widow of Edward de Towcester, c1260-70. Perhaps this was another person of Middle-Eastern origin?

There is no further written evidence showing a Black presence in Northamptonshire until the middle of the sixteenth century. That is not to suggest that Black people were not present in Britain at all. While the royal court had moved from Northampton as the town's economic and political fortunes waned, Black people, notably Africans, continued to be associated with the royal courts in England and Scotland. For example, some were in the service of James IV of Scotland in the early 1500s, mostly as entertainers or musicians, while John Blanke, a Black trumpeter, is pictured in 1511 at the Westminster Tournament celebrating the birth of a son to Henry VIII and Catherine of Aragon. Possibly they had arrived in Britain through Portuguese or other slave trading, or simply as independent travellers.

Saladin – Muslim leader

Eydon Parish Register

Around the middle of the sixteenth century, estate papers, letters, diaries, family portraits and parish records detail the rhythm of ordinary life outside the world of the royal courts and in relatively rural counties like Northamptonshire. It is this type of record that helps us to uncover the hidden history of the Black population in the county. For example, an entry in the Eydon parish registers of 1545 records: "Thomas Bull niger was buried the 16 of December."

As we progress through to the end of the sixteenth century and into the seventeenth century there are more references to Black people in Northamptonshire. This coincides not only with the growing abundance of contemporary written material, but also with changes in taste and fashion, increasing commerce through Britain's expanding merchant fleet, and the beginning of Britain's involvement in the slave trade.

Elizabeth I signalled a change in attitudes towards the small but increasing Black population in Britain when she made attempts to expel "blackmoores brought into this realm, of which kind of people there are already here too many...". It is not clear if her actions arose from simple racism or an attempt to find a scapegoat for the country's ills, either way it contributed to a belief system that saw Black people portrayed at best as an underclass and at worst as subhuman. Such beliefs were gradually to provide the necessary justification for the enslavement of Black Africans. While Elizabeth failed to remove a resilient Black population from England, one or two of her subjects, such as the privateer John Hawkins, realised that African slaves were a profitable commodity. They purchased enslaved people from merchants along the Guinea coast in West Africa (which roughly ran from what is now

Gambia down to Gabon) and sold them mostly to the Spanish on the Caribbean Island of Hispaniola (now Cuba). Some Africans were destined for service in the households of gentry throughout Britain, including Northamptonshire.

By the late sixteenth century it had become quite fashionable in Britain to have a Black slave or servant. In about 1598 Northamptonshire landowner Sir Arthur Throckmorton, who built an estate in Paulerspury, "took into service Anthony, a blackamoor from Guinea". How Anthony came to be in the service of Sir Arthur is perhaps explained by the Throckmorton family connections. Elizabeth Throckmorton, sister of Sir Arthur and a maid of honour to Queen Elizabeth, had secretly married Sir Walter Raleigh. She had been quick to acquire the latest symbol of status via a Captain Clements of Weymouth. Clements had captured at least two slaves from the Spanish. A man named John Hill of Stonehouse, Plymouth, had been imprisoned in the Groyne (the fortified harbour in North

John Speed's map of Northampton, 1610

West Spain now known as La Coruna). On 7 April 1598 he made the following declaration to the Queen: "I was liberated 26 Jan. last, on condition of bringing to the Groyne two Negroes taken by Capt. Clements of Weymouth ... I beg favour for procuring one of the Negroes with Lady Raleigh, that I may speedily return to the Groyne, for which all we poor prisoners shall be grateful."

While Northampton's economic fortunes and political influence had been in decline, the county as a whole was still relatively prosperous. So much so that William Camden was able to write in 1607: "A champion county it is, exceeding populous, and passing well furnished with noblemen and Gentlemen's houses, replenished also with towns and churches, in so much as in some places there are twenty, and in others thirty steeples with spires or square towers within view at once."

Lady Isabella Sackville and her servant

By the middle of the seventeenth century, following the Civil War, wealthy families in the county continued to underline their status by acquiring young Black servants. In the parish register of Castle Ashby, between 1655 and 1661 (the exact year had been omitted): "James Genoue the son of Cassima Genoue born in Sallee in Barbary now aged 23 yeares was baptised into the Christian faith the 5th day of September." It is possible that James Genoue was in service with the Compton family, Earls of Northampton, owners of Castle Ashby. Indeed, there is a portrait dating to c.1650 in the house at Castle Ashby of a Black servant looking up at Lady Isabella, first wife of the third Earl of Northampton. This is probably the earliest visual image of a Black person in Northamptonshire. Not only did the rich employ Black servants, now it became fashionable to have one's portrait adorned by them, replacing or accompanying the favourite family pet. Isabella's left hand rests on the shoulder of her Black servant and is mirrored by the portrait of her husband, whose right hand rests on his favourite dog.

Where the Comptons led, other families such as the Cravens followed. The Winwick parish register for burials in 1674 records: "A Guinean boy, Servt. to Sr. Wm. Craven, baptised ye Summer before & named Winwick, was buried December 17."

Again, this piece of evidence gives us a clue to how the servant came to Northamptonshire: it appears to be as a consequence of Britain's increasing involvement in the slave trade. Like Anthony, the servant of Sir Arthur Throckmorton eighty years earlier, the servant residing in Winwick originated from the slaving coast of Guinea. Sir William Craven had been given the manor of Winwick by his kinsman, William, Lord Craven. This Lord Craven is one of a number of aristocracy and gentry named in a grant made by Charles II to the Company of Royal Adventurers into Africa in 1660, later re-named The Royal Africa Company. It provided an exclusive right to trade in Africa that excluded other British subjects from trading in the region without licence from that Company. To have an interest in such a monopoly was a fast track to riches.

By this time, Britain had started its systematic involvement in the slave trade. This was prompted by the national addiction to sugar (addictions to tea and tobacco were also to have consequences). The British were envious of profits made by Portuguese sugar plantations in Brazil, reliant wholly on the product of 60,000 slaves. The Caribbean islands, notably Barbados, provided the key, with a perfect climate for cultivating sugar. But sugar was notoriously difficult to grow and harvest. It required fourteen months to mature, after which there was only a short period to harvest the crop before it became starch and impossible to mill. Sugar cane therefore required intensive labour, and it was clearly more profitable if you could obtain a cheap and reliable supply, and even better if it were free. Barbados already contained a White population of around 23,000 by mid-century. However, these indentured servants and slaves were regarded as being unreliable and generally unsuited to the climate. The procurement of African slaves to supply the increasing demand for sugar and its by-products, such as rum and molasses, was the obvious answer and led to 20,000 slaves being transported from Africa to Barbados as early as 1655. By 1700 the number of Black slaves in Barbados had grown to around 50,000.

Merchants and gentry in Britain, including Northamptonshire families, were quick to buy into the investment potential. But not every slave was destined for the Caribbean. Some travelled with sea captains or their plantation owners back to Britain, often to fulfil the role of servant and status symbol in the households of the wealthy. The growing number of Black people in Britain is reflected by an increasing number of entries in parish registers of Northamptonshire. An entry in the Guilsborough parish register for baptisms 1683, for example, notes that "A Negroe youth known here by the Name of Titus, was Baptised by ye name of John Jan 3rd. Mr Tho. Ward rector of Ould & Mr. Thomas Hirrick Minister of Harborough & Mrs Anne Butlin Being his witnesses."

Not all Black people in Northamptonshire at this time originated from Africa. Interestingly, in 1688 the Kings Cliffe parish register for baptisms includes: "Marie formerly Called or Sirname Sussanna an Indian woman September the 23". There is a similarity with the entries for John Titus of Guilsborough and James Genoue of Castle Ashby, in that this is an adult baptism. Such baptisms often provide a clue to identifying Black people in early parish registers, where a person's colour or origin is not specified. Adult baptisms in Anglican registers are quite rare and are often a sign that someone has been converted to Christianity, something which many Black servants underwent as their owners sought to "civilize" them. For some slave-owners such baptisms also provided a neat theological justification for their participation in slavery. As part of this process servants were often given anglicised Christian names or, as fashion dictated, classical names such as Titus or Scipio (derived from the Black Roman senator Scipius Africanus). Sometimes they were given surnames that reflected their original African forename. For example Cuffay, a West African forename, was a common surname given to slaves and their descendants.

It becomes easier to identify Black people in parish registers from the late sixteenth century to the first decade of the nineteenth century, where place of origin or ethnicity is noted. Places associated with the slave trade like Guinea are regularly noted, as are terms such as "Niger", "Negro", "Blackamoor" or simply "Black", as demonstrated by the entry in the burial register for Yardley Hastings in 1699, which records: "Black widow was buried December 15th". It would appear that in this corner of Northamptonshire, as in other parts of the county, ethnicity was more important than a name, especially if you were a Black woman.

But it would be wrong to suggest that vicars and parish officers simply made such entries out of curiosity. While ethnicity and place of origin are noted in baptism and burial registers, they occur only occasionally in marriage records, though we know Black people did marry. So why did they add such descriptions?

In Britain, the parish was the main unit of local administration and one important area of responsibility was the relief of the poor. Under the Settlement Laws, a system for distributing relief to the poor, a parish was responsible for its own. To be legally "settled" in a parish, a citizen needed to be born in that parish or work for a master in that parish for a year and a day. If they became destitute then it was in that parish's interest to remove any person who was not "settled" back to his or her parish of origin. Hence, it was important to ensure that parish records carefully noted anything that might be of relevance in the future. Baptisms and burials were the beginning and the end of the cycle of parish administration, but marriages had little bearing on settlement, hence there are fewer additional remarks in marriage registers.

Most of the Black people in Northamptonshire parish records at this time were servants. We should always remember that they were not free. They had been removed from their native land to unfamiliar surroundings and stripped of their name and often their dignity. However, because they had a similar status to the family pet, some were otherwise treated fairly well. Catherine, Lady Rockingham, true to fashion, employed a page at Rockingham Castle whose name was Dobus. Researchers have surmised that he was Black both because of his unusual name and because he received special favours which set him apart from the ordinary servants. We are able to catch a glimpse of his life through the numerous entries in the Household Accounts. In October 1690 it is recorded that £5 and 10 shillings was "Pd. for a little Mare for the Page". Entries are more numerous for 1692 and we can see how he was dressed from top to bottom with the finest clothes. In March an entry reads "Give Dobuss to buy a Hat –/09/–[9 shillings]" and in May "Pd. for 3 yards of fine Shaloon to line the Pages coat –/-7/06" plus "13 yards of gold

Rockingham Castle

Galoon at 5 an ounce for ye Pages coate". For June the task was to make a waistcoat out of "8 yds. of fustian at 16d & 20 yds. at 14d" for Dobus and a fellow servant named Joseph, not forgetting "a pr. of Bootes for Dobuss, 10s". In September the project seems complete with "Dobusse's Sleves" at a cost of 14 shillings and four pence.

A year later and Dobus had clearly grown, so the cycle of clothing him began again. It included shoes, a coat, breeches, stockings and gloves, and was topped off with a "hat wth. Gold edging". By June 1694, still growing, £2 11s was paid to "Mr Drake a coat for ye Page & as by agt. [agreement]".

Catherine, Lady Rockingham died on 21 March 1696. Dobus remained with the family for some time after. However on 4 March 1697 a record relating to Dobus is different from previous entries and has a certain finality. It notes, "Given Dobur who was my Wifes Page 20/-/-[£20]". This would appear to be a final gratuity payment made for his loyal service. What became of Dobus we may never know; perhaps he was set free after the death of his mistress. Certainly it was not uncommon for some favoured Black servants to be given their freedom after years of loyal service.

A notable example of this is the heroic James Chappel of Gretton, Northamptonshire. James Chappel went into the service of the Hattons of Kirby Hall, Northamptonshire in 1663. In 1670 he travelled to Guernsey when Sir Christopher Hatton was made Governor of the Island. An illustration showing Sir Christopher Hatton arriving at Guernsey also depicts James Chappel among the landing party. While in Guernsey, Chappel resided with Hatton and his family at Cornet Castle. It was here that a horrific event took place on the night of the 29 December 1672. During a storm, lightning struck the castle and ignited stores of gunpowder, causing a huge explosion. The Black servant James Chappel bravely rescued Sir Christopher Hatton and his children from the rubble, although Hatton's wife and mother sadly perished. In a deposition of 1727, Chappel, then 82 years old, described the scene after being woken by another servant:

"...it being very darke, they were some time before they could find the door; but at last they gott out, and the first thing this informant then heard was his Lords voice calling for help : and being directed by the voice, this informant (Chappel) at last found he was on the castle wall, and was by his Lordship order'd to go and see for his wife and children ....this informant borrowing a pair of shoes from the soldiers, with some difficulty gott on the Castle Wall, and crep't on his hands and knees to his Lordship where he found him with the mattress and feather-bed under him."

Having saved Hatton, Chappel then describes how he rescued the sisters and children:

"...they found his Lorship's two sisters both alive in bed, but almost suffocated with a beam of the house fallen in betwix't them, and, taking them out, carried them to his Lorship in the Gard-roome ....and on digging about a foot and a half struck on a beam, by the side of which being a little cavity, they open'd it somewhat larger, and, looking in, there saw under the beam ...Miss Anne Hatton, his Lordship's daughter ...and searching further in that cavity, found in another bed there one of the nurses dead, with Miss Margaret Hatton, another of his Lorship's daughters, a child of about one yeare and a half old in her arms playing with a little silver cupp in its hand, and carry'd that to his Lordship, and returning again to the same place, and removing a little more of the rubbish, and a few boards, found in a cradle Elizabeth Hatton."

Despite this tragedy, Hatton remained as Governor in Guernsey until 1680, when he returned to Kirby Hall in Gretton. Hatton died in September 1706 and in his will, proven on 19 February 1707, he made the following bequest: "to my servant James Chapell I give one annuity of twenty pounds a year during the term of his life".

Such a sum enabled Chappel to settle as a free man in Gretton with his wife Elizabeth. Chappel had already established himself in the village when his master visited Kirby Hall while Governor of Guernsey. An entry in the Gretton baptism register relates to "Elizabeth the daughter of James Chapell baptised Sept 10 1676". Unfortunately his daughter survived less than three years, the burial register of the same parish noting: "Elizabeth Chapell buried in Wollen Aug 15 1679".

James Chappel is an outstanding example not only of the hitherto hidden contribution of Black people to British history, but also of the way in which Black people have a long tradition of integrating into local communities. Chappel appears to have married his first wife Elizabeth in St. Martins, Westminster in

1672, the same year as the explosion in Guernsey. Elizabeth died and was buried in Gretton in 1704, and a year later the Gretton parish records report: "James Chappel and Mercy Peach both of this parish married May 7th 1705". It is this union that appears to give rise to another legend surrounding James Chappel, namely that he was the landlord of the Hatton Arms in Gretton, thereby becoming the first Black publican in Northamptonshire. There is no evidence to corroborate this story, but the names of the licensees of the Hatton Arms in Gretton include Thomas Peach (1692-98) and Anna Peach (1701 and 1703), who may have been related to James Chappel's second wife, Mercy Peach. It is perhaps this connection that has evolved into the folklore surrounding James Chappel's association with the Hatton Arms, through generations of oral testimonies from parishioners in Gretton. While they may not have been publicans, James and Mercy continued to live in Gretton and had at least two children, daughter Amey (born in 1706) and son James (born and died in 1714). James Chappel was buried in Gretton on 17 February 1730, followed by Mercy four years later.

Hatton Arms, Gretton

An entry in the Duston parish records of 1700 suggests that James Chappel was not alone as a Black person planting roots in Northamptonshire and starting a family. It notes that "John ye Son of a Blackamore woman was bapt. Janry. 19". As we progress into the eighteenth century, growing numbers of Black people began to settle and start families in Northamptonshire, and were here to stay.

Further Reading:

General:

The Northamptonshire Black History Association's searchable database provides numerous detailed references to the Black presence in Northamptonshire from Medieval times to present, with full details of sources: www.northants-black-history.org.uk

D. Dabydeen, et al (ed.), *The Oxford Companion to Black British History* (Oxford: Oxford University Press, 2007) provides an excellent gateway to many topics and some individuals covered in this chapter, with a detailed bibliography for further reading.

P. Fryer, *Staying Power: The History of Black People in Britain* (London: Pluto Press, 1984) provides the best introduction to the early Black presence in Britain.

S. Schama, *A History of Britain: The British Wars 1603-1776* (London: BBC, 2001) provides a good introduction to Britain's early involvement in the slave trade.

Early communities in Northamptonshire:

There is no single history of Northampton that covers the period discussed in this chapter, but a general introduction can be found in:

H. Cam, *The Borough of Northampton. The Victoria History of the Counties of England* (Northampton: Northamptonshire VCH Trust, 1998)

A. White, *The Story of Northampton*, 1914 (Wakefield: S.R.Publishers, 1970 ed.)

Jewish community:

J. Jolles, *A Short History of the Jews of Northampton 1159-1996* (London: Jolles Publications, 1996)

Parish registers:

K. Chater, 'Hidden from history: Black people in parish records', *Society of Genealogists Magazine*, 26/10 (June 2000)

Primary Sources:

NBHA database (see above)

HMSO Calendar Rolls series provides transcripts of documents held in the National Archives dating from the medieval period to the eighteenth century, including Close Rolls, Pipe Rolls, State Papers (Domestic and Foreign), the Colonial Papers for America and West Indies and records of the Commissioners for Plantations.

C. Markham and J. Cox, (eds.), *Records of the Borough of Northampton*, Vols. 1 and 2 (Northampton: Northampton Corporation, 1898)

Anglican Parish Registers for Northamptonshire: microfiche and originals located at the Northamptonshire Record Office, fiche copies at the Northamptonshire Central Library

Rockingham Castle Household Accounts (Dobus), Lincolnshire Archives, LRO Mon 10/1/A/19

This chapter was written by Terry Bracher

Northamptonshire and India before 1900

European links to India and China extend back thousands of years, and have always depended upon people's desire to travel between these distant places. In the thirteenth century the Italian traveller Marco Polo wrote a famous account of his journey along the Silk Road to China and his visit to South India on the way home. Thirteenth century craftsmen in Exeter Cathedral portrayed a realistic Indian elephant, as travellers' tales began to whet British appetites for a share of the treasures and curiosities of the East. Christopher Columbus was searching for a sea route to India when he arrived instead in the Bahamas in 1492. Six years later Vasco da Gama rounded the Cape of Good Hope and sailed onwards to the Indian port of Calicut. Soon Britain was actively competing with Portuguese, Dutch and French traders for a share of the lucrative Indian and Far Eastern trade in spices, silks and precious stones.

Travellers' tales of the splendid Mughal Empire encouraged Queen Elizabeth to grant a royal charter to the British East India Company in 1600, the last year of her reign. Soon the Company was permitted to set up trading ports and factories, first in Surat (1612), then in Madras (1640), Bombay (1668) and Calcutta (1690). The power and wealth of the East India Company grew spectacularly over the two centuries which followed, while the authority of the Mughal Emperors gradually declined. Britain took advantage of divisions and rivalries among Indian rulers to assert its military as well as economic power. In 1757 Robert Clive's victory at the Battle of Plassey opened the way for the East India Company to seize administrative control of the rich and populous kingdom of Bengal, a key step towards the British government's eventual political rule over the whole of India.

In the late eighteenth century India was seen as a land of golden opportunity by ambitious young men who travelled east, seeking the patronage of the East India Company and hoping for personal wealth. Northamptonshire sent out its share of would-be "nabobs", as successful fortune-hunters were enviously called by their fellow-countrymen. The county also sent British administrators and missionaries who attempted the impossible task of converting India's millions to the Christian religion. During the nineteenth century the British government reined in the greedy excesses of the East India Company, and set about "improving" India as well as systematically exploiting its economic resources. From 1858, after a widespread national uprising against the British, the Company lost its administrative powers. Direct British rule was imposed, and in 1876 Queen Victoria was declared Empress of India. There were plentiful new opportunities in India for the citizens of Northamptonshire, both within the British army and administration and as representatives of British trade and industry.

Meanwhile Indians also began to arrive in Northamptonshire in small but significant numbers. They included some of the rich and famous, as well as poorer Indians who usually came and went unrecorded. This chapter will introduce a number of travellers in both directions, as well as illustrating the influence of India and China upon Northamptonshire homes.

Northamptonshire Fortune-Hunters

John Lloyd Booth of Glendon Hall, near Kettering, set out for India in 1766, as the East India Company was at the climax of the uncontrolled dash for cash which followed its conquest of Bengal. On the evidence of his letters home, John was a greedy as well as adventurous young man. His account of the long, dangerous voyage to India included eager expectations of financial reward: "the many instances of Gentlemen going home in this year's ships who came out about 3 or 4 years ago, now possessed of sixty or seventy Thousand pounds, sufficiently convinces me that should I enjoy my health...I might with

Glendon Hall

a little application succeed to my desires". In another letter he recalled "Lord Cullen's expression upon my taking leave of him: that a man had nothing to do in India but to roll, and the gold would stick to him".

Unfortunately John Lloyd Booth's hopes were soon dashed by Robert Clive's illness and a consequent regime change within the East India Company. Early in 1767 he responded to this delay by starting to "do a little Business for myself. I have purchased a 6th part of another Chinaman's Cargo and am disposing of my Bargain very fast." His investment reminds us that British trade with India was often closely linked to China, where the East India Company hoped to repeat its success in dominating trade upon its own favourable terms. A few months later the young man was still waiting for his big break, dabbling in small-scale trading with the help of an enterprising Indian go-between who "would be for it himself, but I fancy they are not permitted to trade".

Spirits seem to have flagged as temperatures soared with the onset of the hot season. There was a distinctly nostalgic tone to his request for a chest from Glendon, containing items such as "landscape prints", "a large investment of books", and "any Seeds which you think with a little attention grow in this country...I should be very fond of making Experiments if strawberries might thrive here." By April 1767 Calcutta was beginning to "grow excessive hot", and after this date John Lloyd Booth's letters cease. Northamptonshire records reveal his premature death, probably as a victim of the heat and disease which were every Englishman's worst enemy in India. During the eighteenth century more than half of the civil servants appointed to Bengal apparently died there, while in Bombay it was said that "Two monsoons are the life of a man".

Allen Edward Young from Orlingbury, Northamptonshire, was one of the lucky survivors of the eighteenth century Indian trade. Born in 1759 to family of land-owning gentry, he benefited from having an uncle already established within the East India Company when he arrived in India in 1782. By this date Warren Hastings was in power as the reforming Governor General of Bengal, and Allen was confident of his patronage. His Indian career lasted over six years, producing a flow of cheerful correspondence to a younger sister at home. Allen Young later succeeded to his Northamptonshire estate, married a Berkshire lady, produced eight children, and died peacefully at Maidwell before being buried in his native village. His early Indian letters described an East India Company salary starting at "above three hundred pounds per annum". Nine months later, "My situation in point of emolument is not unsatisfactory and I hope in time to accomplish all my wishes".

Like John Lloyd Booth before him, Allen Young had no idealistic vision of remaining in India for the good of that country or for the sake of the British Empire. A few years of Indian trading and administration

Souvenir Horoscope

could set a man up for life back in Britain, and offered a financial opportunity not to be missed. Allen enthusiastically joined Calcutta's hectic social scene whenever he got the opportunity, but his thoughts often turned to "my native home, to the society of my dearly beloved Relations and Friends". He confided to his sister that the most serious disadvantage of Indian life was a lack of prospective marriage partners, begging her to look out for "a Girl in the Circle of your Acquaintance possessed of all the good Qualities...I should be sorry to enter into a Contract of this Nature here for many obvious Reasons." His marriage was in fact delayed until after his return to England, eventually happening when he was forty-five years old. We do not know whether Allen Young had meanwhile gathered in, then abandoned, one or more Indian "wives", as was the British custom of the times.

Allen Young's Indian sojourn was sometimes enlivened by the presence of British visitors, including a young cousin called Charles Boddam. This man's diary of a leisurely tourist trip through Bengal in 1785 is preserved at the Northamptonshire Record Office. It reveals the pampered lifestyle to which successful Englishmen in India had already become accustomed. Charles's aim was "to satisfy my curiosity by seeing some of the principal stations of this opulent country from whence so much wealth flows into Britain". From August to December, his journey passed smoothly with just enough adventures to keep it exciting. Highlights included a visit to Plassey ("every Englishman who comes here must feel a pleasing sensation"); royal entertainment from the Nawab of Bengal ("the fireworks...far surpassed anything of the kind I had seen before"); and an overland journey in the company of 1000 troops with

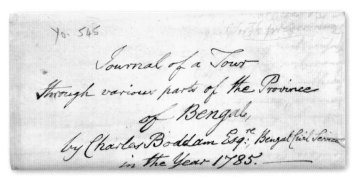

Charles Boddam's Journal

their animals and camp followers. The diary's final paragraphs state the author's comfortable view that "All the idle tales of cruelty and oppression exercised in India by Englishmen are fabricated at home to depreciate and distress the Company... There is not a set of people in the world who enjoy more ease and happiness than those natives who are under the British government." The severe famines afflicting many parts of Bengal had evidently not spoilt this wealthy traveller's pleasant journey.

Northamptonshire Empire-Builders

British rule in India was founded on trade, but also generated huge extra revenue from taxation and gifts. By the end of the eighteenth century it was clear that the East India Company must be more closely supervised by the British government in order to gain wealth for the British nation as well as for greedy individuals. Political controls grew from the 1780s onwards, one trigger being the Company's failure to prevent thousands of deaths from starvation in over-taxed Bengal. British government through the East India Company was gradually regularised, and made more accountable to the British Parliament. But India continued to suffer systematic exploitation of its economic assets, designed to turn it into a leading exporter of raw materials and eventually a leading market for British industrial goods. Among the casualties of British rule were India's own manufacturing industries, including ship-building and metal working as well as the textiles production for which the country had so long been famous.

The nineteenth century government of India required growing numbers of professional administrators and technical experts, though the number of British settlers remained small alongside an Indian rural population of many millions. One of this new, more hard-working breed of empire-builders was Cornwallis Cartwright, younger son of an old Northamptonshire landed family who lived at Aynho House, near Brackley. His career in India spanned thirty years, from his arrival as a junior member of the Bengal civil service in 1820 up to his retirement and return to Britain as a senior judge in 1850. The days of instant "nabob" fortunes were over, and young Cartwright struggled under a load of debt during his early years in India. He never learned to like the country which he helped to rule, and his letters home to his father were often miserable and complaining.

As a young man, Cornwallis seems to have been tempted, like John Lloyd Booth before him, to supplement his salary with unofficial trading. However a first visit to China in November 1822 brought "no chance of a fall", as it coincided with a disastrous fire at the East India Company's cotton warehouses in Canton. The Chinese were stubbornly resisting British trade, and this was reflected in public hostility as well as the probable arson attack on British property. With unconscious irony, Cornwallis observed: "They are most rigid in their own affairs, and affect to be so far superior to the rest of the world both in learning and mechanism as never to be astonished at the production of any foreign specimen of Art... The children are brought up with the idea that we are intruders, both as to Country and Wealth, and are sent by their parents to teaze and plague one while walking along the streets." There was grudging respect in his comment that the Chinese were "very independent, cunning people" and "clever, to an astonishing degree"; but his unfriendly reception and lack of economic success made him impatient to return to India. It took the Opium Wars of 1839-42 and 1856-60 to force open Chinese trade and secure British access through the port of Hong Kong.

In later life Cornwallis Cartwright had less need to beg financial aid from his father. There were happier letters, for example when he described the "splendour and magnificence" of the Hyderabad Residency, where he achieved a lucky promotion to "a Salary of about 2000 Rupees per month" after a colleague's death from cholera. But Cornwallis remained a pessimistic correspondent, doing his duty for the sake of his salary. In 1827 he sent home a martyred account of a recent expedition: "You can have no idea of the vexations, of the horrors of a campaign at this season of the year. The wind blows one continued flame night and day and no earthly contrivance can shut it from one's tent." As late as 1844, he was still trying to escape from India at the earliest possible opportunity: "if I can only find myself once more in dear old Aynho's walls, with an independence in my pocket, and all my family around me, I shall have reached what I have ever considered the height of worldly happiness."

British rule in India was upheld by military power and exercised through economic and administrative systems, but also reinforced by the arrival of British missionaries and educators throughout the nineteenth century. One of the first missionaries in Bengal was William Carey, a Northamptonshire man who set sail for India in 1793 and eventually died there in 1834 after more than forty years continuous effort to master Indian languages and Christianise the natives. His life history has been fully recorded and is still celebrated by the Baptist Church to which he belonged. It offers an impressive tale of one man's rise from humble village origins to a position of eminence and influence.

William Carey was born in Piddington in 1761. Following his baptism in the River Nene, he was appointed as pastor to the chapel at Moulton, where he also ran a school and continued his trade of shoe-making. His first book, published in 1792, argued a detailed case for establishing Baptist missions overseas. Local ministers gathered at Kettering to launch a Missionary Society, and the following year William Carey was the first volunteer to take on the task of converting India. At this time the East India Company refused to sanction missionary work which would antagonise members of the main Indian religions, so his early work was based in the Danish settlement of Serampore.

WILLIAM CAREY.

William Carey

Carey's Moulton cottage and memorial plaque

Conversions were few, but William persisted in his work over the decades, translating the Bible into Bengali and other languages and setting up his own "native schools" and printing press. Gradually the British government recognised the benefits of his work for British rule. In 1801 he was appointed as the first Professor of Sanskrit, Bengali and Mahratta at Fort William College in Calcutta, and from 1813 onwards the East India Company allowed missionaries to work all over British India. By 1834 William Carey had helped found twenty-six more Baptist missions. His life is commemorated by a marble tablet in Moulton Chapel, and by a little museum in the nearby cottage where he lived.

Other Northamptonshire empire-builders included members of the Northamptonshire Regiment who served many tours of duty in various parts of India throughout the period of British rule. Their contribution, and that of Northamptonshire businessmen, is described in Chapter Five.

Indian Visitors and Settlers in Northamptonshire

Empire-builders have received much more recognition in British history books than the Indians whose arrival in this country was an equally noteworthy outcome of the British rule. The number of Indian visitors and settlers is uncertain, but it is clear that they travelled here for a wide variety of reasons. India became a source of cheap labour from an early stage, and from the seventeenth century onwards many Indians came to Britain as sailors and servants, as well as being despatched to other corners of the British Empire to work plantations, build roads and railways, or serve the British Army. Those who arrived here with their British employers sometimes found it hard to survive, let alone to return home, and their harsh situation was acknowledged by the Victorian provision of charitable London shelters for "Asiatic seamen" and "ayahs" (nannies). More fortunate Indians arrived voluntarily with the aim of studying or setting up businesses. As the historian Rozina Visram points out, "by the time South Asians began arriving in Britain in larger numbers in the 1950s there was already a sizeable resident Indian community".

As an inland county, Northamptonshire received fewer visitors and had less Indian residents than some other parts of the country. Nevertheless there is occasional evidence in the local press and elsewhere of an Indian presence, whether as servants, entertainers or pedlars or (later in the nineteenth century) as professional men. A few Indian servants appear in the parish registers, alongside larger numbers of African origin. An Indian woman was baptised in Kings Cliffe in 1688, and a seven-year-old native of Bengal christened at Blatherwycke in 1714. Indian jugglers performed at Northampton Town Hall in 1818. Arthur Mee's history of Northamptonshire records a lone Indian pilgrim found travelling on foot from Liverpool towards William Carey's birthplace in the 1840s; a tradition followed up by several twentieth century Indian Christians who have also made the long journey to his Moulton chapel.

Indian doctors are discussed in Chapter Five. A more entrepreneurial branch of medicine was practised by visiting Indian "oculists" who found themselves on trial for "obtaining money by false pretences" at the Central Criminal Court in 1893. Northamptonshire witnesses played a crucial part in this trial, offering evidence that the treatment received from the Indians in Kettering and Wellingborough had been far more effective than previous interventions based upon conventional medicine. In one case the "oculist" had successfully removed a cataract from a Wellingborough man's right eye: "it was just like a transformation scene to him. He had not seen daylight for seven years, and after the operation he could see all over the room." The trial ended in a triumphant acquittal of the prisoners.

In contrast to these obscure and barely recorded Indians, a large amount of information is available on two more famous visitors to Northamptonshire. Marharajah Duleep Singh was deposed as the Sikh ruler of the Punjab in 1849. Sent to England for education and political safe-keeping, the handsome young prince was soon a great favourite with Queen Victoria and spent several holidays with her family at Osborne House in the Isle of Wight. When she handed him the Koh-I-Noor diamond during a portrait sitting, he returned it to her with a speech of graceful loyalty. In later life he became disillusioned with British rule in India, reverted to Sikhism and unsuccessfully petitioned to be allowed to return to the Punjab. By this date he had also established himself as an English gentleman with a Norfolk country estate. Duleep Singh's family often travelled through Northamptonshire when they visited their estate. On 1 January 1908 the *Northampton Mercury* reported that his son and daughter had visited the crypt at Rothwell, lunched in Kettering and motored on to Oundle for an overnight stay. Daughters Sophia and Catherine Duleep Singh became well-known supporters of the women's suffrage movement, but the Northamptonshire press continued to honour the family as visiting royalty.

The admiration shown for "exotic" Indian princes was in stark contrast to the prejudice experienced by most other Indians in Victorian Britain. Even within the royal court, Victoria sometimes had to defend her Indian servants and teachers against jealous criticism. Highly educated, wealthy Indians found themselves excluded from certain professional bodies and from the inner circles of upper class society.

The Indian Uprising of 1857 (known in Britain as the Indian Mutiny) was put down amid atrocities and bloodshed which reinforced racial prejudice and fed the long-standing belief that the British were morally superior to those they ruled. From the 1880s there was a growing fear of organised, peaceful Indian nationalism. The Indian National Congress was formed in 1885 to demand a larger role for Indians in the government of their own country. One of its founding members and early Presidents was the Parsi scholar and businessman Dadabhai Naoroji.

Dadabhai Naoroji

This remarkable man left his impression upon the history of Northamptonshire, as well as that of India and Britain. He has been fondly called the "Grand Old Man of India", and is viewed today as an architect of the Indian freedom struggle. British rule had brought a number of benefits to India, but in the political arena Naoroji witnessed many pledges being breached which led him to claim that "thus treating the natives of India not as British subjects...ensured a political drain from India to England". This drain included Naoroji himself, who was elected to the British Parliament in 1892 as the Liberal party candidate for Central Finsbury and the first British Indian MP. He remained true to his fellow-countrymen and women, and summed up their feelings by saying: "The natives call the British system 'Sakar ki Churi', the knife of sugar. That is to say, there is no oppression, it is all smooth and sweet, but there is the knife, notwithstanding." In other words, power and control often overrode fair play and justice.

Dadabhai Naoroji played an important part in winning fellow-Liberals as supporters of Indian reform, among them Northampton's famous Radical MP Charles Bradlaugh. In 1883 Bradlaugh used a public meeting at Northampton's Guildhall to denounce the iniquities of British rule over the previous century, and to demand progress towards Indian self-rule within the British Empire. Naoroji himself came to Northampton to address the public on the same theme five years later, bringing with him Womesh Chandra Bonnerjee, President of the Indian National Congress. The Mayor

Charles Bradlaugh statue

of Northampton welcomed both men to a packed Guildhall, where the two distinguished Indians addressed the Northampton public on "India's Wrongs and English Remedies". Womesh Bonnerjee told the audience: "India has become bound up with you...It is necessary for the peace of both countries...that some method should be devised by which the people will be more contented, the people will get more to eat (cheers), the people will be able to discharge the duties of citizenship." Charles Bradlaugh solemnly asked his Northampton constituents to support him as he took on the mighty responsibility of representing India in the British Parliament. The following year he travelled to Bombay and visited the Indian National Congress in person. Bradlaugh's status as the "Member for India" is recorded to the present day on his statue in Abington Square, Northampton.

Charles Bradlaugh statue inscription

India and China in Northamptonshire Homes

Indians have culturally enriched British society over many centuries through food and fashion. Indian curries are now more popular than fish and chips. Indian influences upon fashions in clothes and jewellery are also a huge success. The British are beautifying their bodies with long, flowing cotton and silk fabrics and colourful beaded and gemmed jewellery. What was once available only for the very rich is today's fashion for the majority as a colourful personal and aesthetic statement.

Many British homes are nowadays influenced by the wealth of and luxury feel of Indian and Chinese fabrics. Current home furnishing trends include silk and sequinned cushions, embroidered silk or brocade curtains, plush wool carpets and fabric sofas. This "ethnic" or "oriental" look has in fact influenced interior decoration in Britain since the early sixteenth century. When most of the British population were living in cold, draughty stone houses, only the elite and rich could afford the elegance of wall art, and the warmth and beauty of silk fabrics and wool carpets imported from the East.

Country houses in Northamptonshire contain many examples of the appeal of oriental crafts and images. Canons Ashby has an eighteenth century plaster portrait of an Indian princess. Kelmarsh Hall has early nineteenth century wall paper hand-painted by artists in China. Deene Park and Althorp House contain beautiful oriental china and furniture. However it is Boughton House we shall now explore in more detail.

Boughton House

Boughton House has been the home of the Montagu family and their descendants since 1528. This family were leading landowners in England and Scotland who invested in the slave economy of the West Indies, travelled extensively in Europe, and ornamented their house with the most beautiful furnishings and paintings which money could buy.

In 1624 the Governors of the Dutch East India Company instructed their factory at Surat in India "to purchase 540 Persian carpets of high quality or if better quality and lower cost, the same of Indian examples and 300 Persian ones". Here is an example of an early wool rug from Lahore, Northern India.

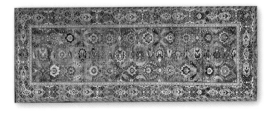

Boughton House retains in the family collection both oriental and occidental pile-knotted carpets made before 1800. It is likely that these were purchased by Ralph, first Duke of Montagu, with bills for cleaning confirming their presence in the house between 1695 and 1705. This collection of carpets is described in Dr Murdoch's book on Boughton House: "The Boughton carpets represent the most significant group of pile weavings, and for the most part eastern pile weavings, to have survived in the collection of one family. As such, they are a wonderful, if poignant, reminder of the riches which once adorned the floors of many great houses in sixteenth and seventeenth century Britain, but which have now disappeared."

Boughton 1585 carpet

Inspiration for the carpets at Boughton House may have come from the many other oriental carpets in Tudor England at the time, Henry VIII having over eight hundred carpets of his own! Spain was weaving carpets with Turkish designs from at least the fifteenth century. There are four European rugs at Boughton with Turkish designs, three with the "star" Ushak (West Anatolia) and one with the Arabesque design. The three star carpets all bear the Montagu coat of arms and seem to have been woven for the marriage of the third Sir Edward Montagu in 1585. They are extremely unusual and different in construction, if not design, to both Persian and Indian carpets of the period and European manufactured ones. It is thought that the carpets were woven in either Norwich or Yorkshire, but no significant evidence is available to prove their true provenance.

The wool rug shown below is known as the Buccleuch Sanguszko and is the most important of the Safavid Persian carpets at Boughton, as one of only two of its type in this country. It is a glorious mixture of Islamic and Chinese influences. The flying cranes in the pink and green field cartouches and the dragon and phoenix combats in the main border of the carpet are characteristic of Safavid woven art at its peak.

Wool rug from Central Persia

There are seven other Persian rugs at Boughton, though not all are always on display. Two are silk and known as Polonaise (or Polish) as they were originally thought to be from the country rather than imported through it. The other five are often described as Indo-Persian or Indo-Esfahan. Disagreement continues over the exact origin of these type of carpets.

The difficulty of attributing artefacts from the past can also be illustrated by two eighteenth century lacquer cabinets, previously considered Dutch, English, German, Chinese and Japanese but now thought to be Japanese craftsmanship altered or repaired in England. They are exotic pieces, being white rather than the normal red, green or black lacquer work.

The white Chinese porcelain at Boughton House is thought to have been collected by the Duchess of Marlborough and gifted to her daughter on her marriage to the second Duke of Montagu in 1703. It is known in the West as Blanc de Chine and named in China as Dehua ware, after the town in the Southern Coastal Province of Fujian where it is still made. This porcelain was made in huge quantities for the West and many European collections contain similar pieces.

Illustrated are a Buddha figure and the two ladies are representations of the Bodhisattva Guanyin

(Goddess of Mercy), often misinterpreted in the West as the Virgin Mary. Originally many of these pieces would have been brightly painted and traces of the pigmentation can still be seen on some of those at Boughton House.

Blanc de Chine Buddah

Blanc de Chine ladies

The portrait of Mary Churchill, Duchess of Montagu, in oriental costume was painted by Charles Jervas (c.1675-1739). Her choice of costume was fanciful rather than authentic, but again illustrates the admiration of wealthy British families for "exotic" eastern styles and fabrics. When the Montagus built themselves a summer pavilion, they chose a Chinese tent ornamented with dragons. This prized possession was displayed at their London home before being brought to Boughton House.

It can be seen from the all the above examples how influential the East has been on lifestyles in this country. Yet often little acknowledgement is given to eastern culture, whether in British history books or by present-day British society.

Duchess of Montagu in Eastern attire

Chinese Pavilion roof detail, Boughton House

Further Reading:

S. Ashton, *The British in India: From Trade to Empire* (London: Batsford,1987)

P. Bance, *The Duleep Singhs* (Stroud: Sutton Publishing, 2004)

J. Bush, *Moving On: Northamptonshire and the Wider World* (Northampton: Nene Publications, 1989)

S.Carey, *A Life of William Carey, Baptist Missionary* (London: Marshall, Morgan and Scott, 1936)

P. Fryer, *Black People in the British Empire: An Introduction* (London: Pluto Press, 1984)

L. James, *Raj. The Making and Unmaking of British India* (London: Little, Brown and Company, 1977)

P. Lawson, *The East India Company* (London: Longman, 1993)

A. Mee, *The King's England. Northamptonshire: County of Spires and Stately Homes* (London: Hodder and Stoughton, 1945)

T. Murdoch (ed.), *Boughton House: The English Versailles* (London: Faber and Faber, 1992)

R. Visram, *Ayahs, Lascars and Princes* (London: Pluto Press, 1986)

R. Visram, *Asians in Britain. 400 Years of History* (London: Pluto Press, 2002)

Primary Sources:

Northamptonshire Record Office
Booth of Glendon papers in Gompertz (Glendon) collection
Young (Orlingbury) collection
Cartwright (Aynhoe) collection

Northamptonshire Central Library
Biographical and Literary Notes of William Carey D.D. (London: Alexander Shepheard, 1886)

Moulton
William Carey Museum
Baptist Chapel

Boughton House
Guide Book and website: www.boughtonhouse.org.uk
Information provided by Charles Lister, House Manager

NBHA database
The Northamptonshire Black History Association's searchable database gives detailed references to local sources of evidence on the Indian visitors included in the chapter: www.northants-black-history.org.uk

This chapter was written by Wajiha Mohammad and Julia Bush

Black Servants and Slaves

The origins of the British transatlantic slave trade were described in Chapter One. With royal encouragement, slave traders made their fortunes by trafficking men, women and children from the West African coast to the British Caribbean colonies. British manufactured goods, including firearms, were sold to the wealthier Africans to raise the resources needed to capture or purchase slaves. Enslaved Africans fetched high prices in the Caribbean as the expanding sugar plantations demanded more and more labour. The highest profits of all could be made from the booming export trade from the Caribbean to Britain, where slave-grown sugar was used to sweeten tea, coffee and hot chocolate drinks as well as becoming a staple part of British food. Other important exports included logwood (used for dyeing), cotton and tobacco. This Triangular Trade was well-established by the end of the seventeenth century, and had already begun to increase the number of Black people in Britain. Planters and slave traders who did not want to take their enslaved domestic servants back with them to the Caribbean were only too willing to sell them on to new British masters who saw Black slaves as fashionable ornaments and accessories. They were also a symbol of Britain's power in the world.

This chapter continues the story of Black servants and slaves into the eighteenth century, when the British slave trade reached its peak. By the end of the century the Black population of this country had reached an estimated 20,000. The leading slave ports of London, Bristol and Liverpool had the largest number of Black inhabitants, but there is evidence of a growing Black presence in every county of England as well as many parts of Wales, Scotland and Ireland. Many Black people had already achieved freedom from slavery by various means, and were successfully shaping their own lives and communities. Meanwhile the profits of British slavery were immense. Out of more than twelve million Africans shipped across the Atlantic, nearly three million travelled in British ships. By the late eighteenth century more than 60 per cent of the British trade was based at Liverpool, where the decade from 1783-93 saw a slavery income of over £12 milllion, from 878 voyages and the sale of 300,000 slaves. The benefits of this wealth rippled out across the British economy, helping to finance the Industrial Revolution as well as many grand buildings and famous British institutions.

Northamptonshire had its share of families who profited directly or indirectly from slavery. In the Northamptonshire Record Office, evidence of the county's links to the slave trade lies buried within estate papers. As early as 1670 Thomas Herbert, who later became the Duke of Grafton's land steward, helped a fortune-seeking Englishman called Ambrose Bennett to establish a small plantation in Jamaica. Bennett planned to employ six enslaved "negro" men and women and four indentured White servants to produce "cacao", the basis for the hot chocolate drunk in Britain. Fifty years later the Duke of Montagu, owner of Boughton House, committed himself to a much more ambitious investment. A total of £40,000 was spent on an expedition to St Lucia which aimed to settle a White population on the island as well as to secure a private monopoly of its trade in slave-grown sugar. Parliamentary records show that the British government sanctioned this exercise in licensed risk-taking. But a written account by Captain Nathaniel Uring, which survives in the library at Boughton House, reveals that the expedition became a costly short-term failure.

Though the profits from slavery could be enormous, the dangers of seeking a Caribbean fortune were also considerable. Ambrose Bennett died of fever in Jamaica in 1672. The Duke of Montagu lost part of his fortune in St Lucia, but was not deterred from later, more successful investments in the slave economy. Meanwhile many poorer Northamptonshire men found themselves playing a direct role in the British slave trade without having chosen to do so. The Northamptonshire Regiment was formed in 1741 and over the next two hundred years helped to build and defend the British Empire around the globe. In the Regimental Museum in Abington Park, Northampton, we learn of the heavy casualties suffered by ordinary soldiers as they garrisoned Caribbean islands and put down slave rebellions.

Black servants in Northamptonshire stately homes were also conscripts, usually with even fewer alternatives open to them than the poor White soldiers and sailors caught up in the British slave trade. The fact that many were indulged as family "pets" did not make them free, though it might sometimes lead to a relatively comfortable lifestyle. A number of local sources show the "privileged" treatment of favourite servants. At Boughton House, as well as at Rockingham Castle, ledger books record various items of expenditure linked to individual servants. In 1727-8, soon after the failed St Lucia expedition, entries concerning "Charles the Black" include purchase of a velvet cap, nursing in sickness, payment of a footman's wage, and even some schooling. A list of household instructions states that "the black boy" is to have the privilege of a maid's laundry services. "The Black of Her Grace" was further honoured by being included in a portrait of his mistress, Lady Mary Churchill, Duchess of Montagu. This portrait, painted by Enoch Seaman in the 1720s, shows a well-dressed and serious-faced young man, apparently kneeling beside his mistress as he holds the skein of embroidery silk which she is winding ready for use.

*Duchess of Montagu
and Charles the Black*

Other portraits including Black servants can be found at Castle Ashby, Lamport Hall and Althorp House. Some of these paintings were completed and purchased abroad and therefore do not show local people. However in other cases the individual Black servants can again by identified by name, and linked to evidence from written sources. This portrait is one of two at Althorp which show Caesar Shaw. His baptism in 1732 is recorded in the Great Brington parish register. The painting shows him attending John Spencer and his nephew John, later first Earl Spencer. He is placed in a lowly position alongside a favourite dog, but is nevertheless portrayed as a strong, handsome adult figure whose servile posture enhances the status of his masters.

The significance of sixteenth and seventeenth century parish register entries was discussed in Chapter One. There was much continuity into the eighteenth century, for example in the naming practices related to Black servants. Baptised children continued to be robbed of their birth names, as well as of their families, friends and African culture. Preferred baptismal names often combined a Christian saint with a Roman hero: for example Charles Bacchus was baptised at Haselbech in 1754 and Peter Alexander Sambo at Horton House in 1773. In the latter case the baptism was a particularly grand affair, the sponsors being the Viscount and Viscountess Hinchingbrooke together with their friend and neighbour the Honourable William Augustus Montagu. Eight-year-old "Peter" survived

Caesar Shaw and his masters

only two more years in Northamptonshire, his burial being recorded on 15 January 1775. Child deaths were not unusual in the eighteenth century, but we should remember these child servants as among the saddest victims of the British slave trade as well as recipients of favours from their masters.

Only a small number of servants were granted a tombstone, and very few of these have survived to the present day. In the churchyard at Culworth we can still read of the esteem earned by Charles Bacchus during his short life as a servant to the Bond family, who owned plantations in Jamaica:

Charles Bacchus gravestone

In Memory of CHARLES BACCHUS (an African) Who died March 31 1762. He was beloved and Lamented by the Family he Serv'd, Was Grateful and Humane and gave hopes of Proving a faithful Servant a Good Man. Aged 16.
Here trifles cease, Ambitions oer.
And Slave of Monarch is no more.
The Good alone will find in Heav'n
Rewards assigned, and Honours giv'n.

A much later tombstone, dating from the final years before British slavery was legally abolished, records a remarkable debt of gratitude to a Black servant. Anthony Williams was employed by the O'Brien family of Blatherwycke. In 1836 he sacrificed his life as he rescued his master from drowning in a local lake. His action rivalled the heroism shown by James Chappel of Gretton, more than 150 years earlier. It was recorded for posterity in the sentimental language of the contemporary British anti-slavery campaign:

Blatherwycke church

His home far off in the broad Indian main
He left to rid himself of slavery's chain.
Friendless and comfortless he passed the sea,
On Albion's shores to seek for liberty.
Yet vain his search for aye with toiling brow
He never found his freedom until now.

It is very unlikely that Anthony Williams was treated as a slave when he arrived in Britain. He is more likely to have been a refugee from Caribbean slavery, judging from this verse. Yet enslaved people were bought and sold in eighteenth century Northamptonshire. On 20 December 1731 the *Northampton Mercury* carried the following advertisement: "Any Gentleman, etc. That are willing to purchase a Negro Boy, just come to England, about ten Years of Age, may enquire of Dr. Jennings of Hanslope, or of the Printer hereof."

Any Gentleman, &c. that are willing to purchase a Negro Boy, just come to England, about ten Years of Age, may enquire of Dr. Jennings of Hanslope, or of the Printer hereof.

Newspaper advertisement 1731

Towards the end of the eighteenth century, the legal status of slavery was increasingly under attack. The story of the anti-slavery movement belongs to the next chapter, but it should be noted here that most of the leading Black opponents of slavery were former servants, and many had themselves been enslaved. Legal challenges to slavery within Britain were repeatedly launched in the British courts from the 1770s onwards. These generally related to the plight of enslaved Black servants who had escaped from their masters then been recaptured. Such cases often came to the attention of White sympathisers through the vigilance of the Black abolitionists.

The most famous legal case was that of James Somerset, enslaved in Jamaica and threatened with deportation back to slavery in 1772. Lord Justice Mansfield eventually ruled against his deportation, though not against slavery itself. His judgement was delivered in court to an audience which included many of Somerset's supporters. According to the *London Chronicle* the Black people present "bowed with profound respect to the Judges, and shaking each other by the hand, congratulated themselves upon their recovery of the rights of human nature, and their happy lot that permitted them to breathe the free air of England". Later, a celebration party was attended by over two hundred Black Londoners.

It is thought that Mansfield may have been influenced by the presence of an educated and beautiful Black woman within his own household. Dido Elizabeth Lindsay was the illegitimate daughter of his nephew and a companion rather than a servant to his other young female relatives. In his will the Judge granted her financial support for life as well as confirming her legal freedom. Meanwhile her cousin and childhood friend Elizabeth Finch-Hatton had married into the Northamptonshire aristocracy, living at Kirby Hall in the early nineteenth century. Perhaps Dido visited her there, after her own wedding to a London businessman.

Dido and Lady Elizabeth Murray

Other legal records provide additional information about the status and lifestyle of Black servants in eighteenth century Britain. The transcripts of Old Bailey trials from 1674 to 1834 are now available online, and include over thirty cases related to "negros" accused of crimes or victims of crime. Sometimes, servants seized their freedom and their master's or mistress's property at the same time. Perhaps they felt they were owed as much after years of unpaid or under-paid domestic labour. In other cases they were found guilty of pick-pocketing or burglary, or stole small items on impulse. Punishments for theft were severe, consisting often of seven years' transportation to a penal colony even for thieves as young as fourteen years old.

There were, however, more legitimate routes to freedom. Ignatius Sancho is probably the most famous Black servant who lived for part of his life in eighteenth century Northamptonshire. Born on a slave ship and orphaned at an early age, he could scarcely have had a less promising start. When he arrived in Britain in 1731, he was enslaved to three sisters who tried to guarantee his obedience by denying him an education. Fortunately young Sancho's enthusiasm for self-improvement became known to the Duke of Montagu, who had a town house in nearby Blackheath and a benevolent interest in African intelligence. Soon the Duke took over his education and his employment, and as an adult Sancho developed into a promising writer and composer as well as a trusted butler. After many years of service in London and Northamptonshire, he was granted his freedom and an annual allowance. This was sufficient to fund a London grocer's shop, where Ignatius Sancho raised his family and entertained his literary friends as well as earning a modest living selling the produce of the British colonies. These friends included Dr Samuel Johnson, who authored the first English dictionary. Johnson's servant Francis Barber was another talented Black man who so impressed his employer that he received an inheritance, enabling him to lead an independent life as a married man and village school teacher.

The well-recorded life histories of a small number of exceptional men should not be allowed to obscure the achievements of other Black servants who worked for and won their freedom. In Northamptonshire there are intriguing shreds of evidence which help us to build up a more varied and interesting picture of servants' lives. Some, at least, succeeded in escaping from servitude through their own efforts rather than through the patronage of their employers. The Northamptonshire Record Office holds a rare sequence of letters relating to the disappearance of "Cesar Montague" in 1755. In November 1754

Cesar himself wrote to the Countess of Cardigan soliciting a post at Boughton House and thanking her for past favours. He had apparently been dismissed from employment as a carpenter in nearby Kettering, a job for which he displayed little liking or aptitude. It seems likely from his fine handwriting that this young man had been among the "pampered" child servants, but that he had perhaps fallen out of favour or simply grown too old to serve as a page-boy and personal attendant. Instructions were issued for the former servant to go to Boughton, but a few weeks later another letter commented that "Cesar has still not been heard of". Had Cesar Montague decided to take his fortune into his

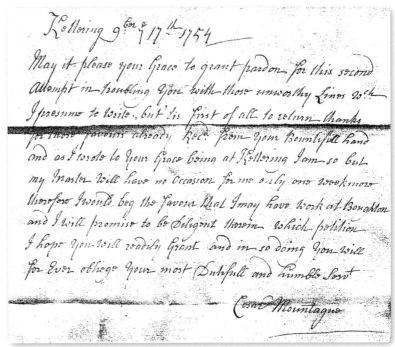

Cesar Montague's letter 1754

own hands and run away to London? The capital city would already have been well-known to him, as he served the daughter and heiress of the Duke and Duchess of Montagu.

London was a natural magnet for the free Black British population, offering both a range of employment and a growing sense of community. However Black servants sometimes made independent lives for

Ignatius Sancho

themselves within Northamptonshire itself. The parish records of Gretton, on the doorstep of the Hatton family's stately home, illustrate how one man gradually settled into village life during the eighteenth century. Richard Dare was identified as a Black man on his burial record. He died in 1770, after fifteen years as the landlord of the Hatton Arms and twenty-one years of marriage to Ann Medwell. The couple had produced a family of four daughters and eight sons, and the records reveal at least two more Dare marriages and ten Dare grandchildren registered in the same village between 1777 and 1797. The Hatton Arms, already linked to the Chappel family in the previous century, seems to have remained in the Dare family for many years after Richard Dare's death. By the end of the eighteenth century the Dares had simply blended into the local population. It is quite possible that their descendants live in Northamptonshire to the present day, without any knowledge of their African ancestors.

Further Reading:

P. Fryer, *Staying Power* (London: Pluto Press, 1984)

HM Government, *Bicentenary of the Abolition of the Slave Trade Act, 1807-2007* (London: Dept for Communities and Local Government, 2007)

A. Hochshild, *Bury the Chains. The British Struggle to Abolish Slavery* (London: Pan Books, 2006)

T. Hosking, *Black People in Britain 1650-1850* (London: Macmillan Education,1986)

R. King, S. Sandhu, J. Walvin and C. Phillips, *Ignatius Sancho. An African Man of Letters* (London: National Portrait Gallery, 1997)

Set All Free, *Setting the Scene for 2007* (London: Churches Together, 2005)

S. Wise, *Though the Heavens May Fall* (London: Pimlico, 2006)

J. Walvin, *A Short History of Slavery* (London: Penguin Books, 2007)

Primary Sources:

Northamptonshire Record Office
Grafton (Wakefield Lodge) collection
Montagu (Boughton) collection
Anglican parish registers for Northamptonshire
Alehouse records for Northamptonshire

Northamptonshire Central Library
Northampton Mercury

Boughton House
N. Uring, A Relation of the Late Intended Settlement of St Lucia and St Vincent (1725)

Gravestones
Culworth and Blatherwycke churchyards

Portraits
Boughton House, Castle Ashby, Lamport Hall, Althorp House

Old Bailey Records
Old Bailey Online: The Proceedings of the Old Bailey 1674-1913,
www.oldbaileyonline.org.uk

The Northamptonshire Black History Association database gives detailed references to local sources of evidence on the Black residents of Northamptonshire included in the chapter: www.northants-black-history.org.uk

This chapter was written by Monica Babb and Julia Bush

The Anti-Slavery Movement

In 1807 Parliament voted to end the British slave trade and in 1838 slavery itself was legally abolished. Commemorations of slave trade abolition have often focused upon events in Parliament, and upon such famous abolitionists as William Wilberforce and Thomas Clarkson. But it should never be forgotten that the longest campaign against slavery was fought by enslaved people themselves.

Direct resistance to transatlantic slavery began in Africa and on board the ships which carried men, women and children towards a future of exploitation and suffering in the Caribbean and the Americas. Many people resisted capture by the slavers, and shipboard revolts were recorded as far back as 1532, when a hundred Africans killed the crew of a Portuguese slave ship and escaped back to the coast of Ghana. The 1839 mutiny on the Amistad, recorded in Steven Spielberg's famous film, was merely one among dozens of acts of desperate resistance. There were over fifty major mutinies during the notorious "Middle Passage", some ending in victory and some in further disaster for those who had already lost everything except life itself. Individuals not infrequently chose starvation or suicide as the final means of escape from slavery.

Resistance continued once the terrible journey was over. Enslaved men and women opposed their masters through small-scale deceit and disobedience, as well as through more dangerous acts of collective defiance. Runaways in Jamaica and other islands formed free Maroon communities in inaccessible mountain areas. Slave revolts, sometimes well-planned and temporarily successful, were a regular feature of Caribbean history throughout the centuries leading up to British slavery abolition. Their contribution towards eventual emancipation is difficult to measure, but should never be underestimated. All forms of resistance helped to make slavery less safe and less profitable, as well as sometimes swaying humanitarian and religious British public opinion in favour of abolition.

Direct and indirect opposition to slavery by enslaved people was also evident in Britain itself. From the early eighteenth century many British newspapers carried advertisements for runaways, as well as "for sale" notices for imported Black servants who were no longer wanted by their masters. As we saw in Chapter Three, the legal status of slaves was under periodic challenge during the eighteenth century. All such legal challenges began with an individual's refusal to submit to his or her master's command. Gradually a growing body of Black and White abolitionists began to mount the organised, continuous campaigns which culminated in legislation against the British slave trade and British slavery.

Northamptonshire played a part in ending, as well as supporting, the transatlantic slave trade. Some of the best-known Black opponents of slavery visited the county, while several prominent White abolitionists were born or settled here. Northamptonshire, with its strong traditions of non-conformist Christianity, offered promising territory for the anti-slavery campaign. Local evidence survives to illustrate each of its main phases.

The first phase, leading up to the 1807 Abolition, lasted throughout the second half of the eighteenth century. American Quakers were to the fore in expressing religious objections to slavery, arguing that all people were equal before God and therefore worthy of humane treatment and Christian education. It took many decades to convince all Quakers to carry this conviction fully into practice by freeing their own slaves, but the anti-slavery message was gradually spread through the American colonies and back to Britain by travelling preachers. In 1772 John Woolman, one of the greatest Quaker writers and travellers, crossed the Atlantic to carry his anti-slavery ministry to Britain. His journal records his visit to the Northampton Quakers. Their Monthly Meeting minute book, now in the Northamptonshire Record Office, tells us that he had a friendly reception here before proceeding on to York, where he died of smallpox a few weeks later. Over the next two decades other American Quakers followed in his footsteps, and British Quaker visitors to the Northampton meeting included several members of well-known abolitionist families.

John Wesley, the founder of Methodism, was among those who read Quaker anti-slavery literature. In 1774 he published his own *Thoughts on Slavery*, which roundly condemned the trade and its consequences. Wesley preached several times in Northamptonshire from 1741 onwards, and by the end of the century Methodist meetings were grouped around Northampton, Higham Ferrers, Towcester and Brackley. The religious opposition to slavery included members of other denominations, most notably the Baptists who were much strengthened by the foundation of the Northamptonshire Baptist Association in 1764. This organisation helped to form the Baptist Missionary Society in the 1790s, source of Northamptonshire missionaries who spread the anti-slavery message across the world as well as bringing it home forcibly to the British government. William Carey's work as the first Baptist missionary in India was described in Chapter Two. His long and distinguished career included heartfelt denunciations of slavery, whether in India or the Caribbean. John Smith of Rothwell and William Knibb of Kettering followed directly in his footsteps, contributing powerfully to the second phase of the anti-slavery campaign.

The late eighteenth century religious opponents of slavery included evangelical Anglicans as well as non-conformists. John Newton, the former slave-ship captain who wrote the hymn "Amazing Grace", was ordained as an Anglican priest in 1764. He published his *Thoughts Upon the African Slave Trade* while living in Olney as a neighbour and friend of the anti-slavery poet William Cowper. One of Cowper's poems neatly summed up the conflict between self-interest and Christian conscience experienced by many British people:

John Newton church window, Olney

> *I own I am shock'd at the purchase of slaves,*
> *And fear those who buy them and sell them are knaves;*
> *What I hear of their hardships, their tortures, and groans,*
> *Is almost enough to draw pity from stones.*
> *I pity them greatly, but I must be mum,*
> *For how could we do without sugar and rum?*

Thomas Clarkson and William Wilberforce, the most famous of all the anti-slavery campaigners, were converted to the cause in the 1780s. These men were influenced by their reading, but also by their encounters with individuals who had a far more direct and painful knowledge of the horrors of the slave trade.

Sansom Occom

One of John Newton's more unusual visitors in Olney was the Native American preacher Sansom Occom. Travelling with a White American pastor, Occom spent two years in Britain (1766-68) and raised £11,000 towards the funding of Dartmouth College. In his diary he recorded large and successful meetings at Kettering and Northampton, as well as Olney. He described Newton as "a minister of the Church of England, he was a sailor, and God marvellously turn'd him and he is a flaming preacher of the Gospel." While in Northampton he stayed with the non-conformists: "in the even'g I Preached at the Meeting House where the great Doc'r Doddridge was Minister... there is a number of warm Christians in this town."

Northamptonshire has direct connections to some of the earliest Black British campaigners against British slavery: Ignatius Sancho, Ottobah Cugoano and Olaudah Equiano. The role of these men in the 1807 abolition was undervalued during their lifetime and neglected by most historians until the recent growth of research into Black British history. Ignatius Sancho's link to the Montagu family of Boughton House, Kettering, was described in Chapter Three. Although he died in 1780, he had already made his mark as a talented African born into slavery who wanted to use his abilities on behalf of his people. In his *Letters*, published in 1782, he aimed to show that "an untutored African may possess abilities equal to a European". His admirers included the Prime Minister, Lord North, and Sancho became an inspiring symbol of Black achievement to later abolitionists.

Ottabah Cugoano was enslaved in West Africa, taken to Grenada, then eventually freed by his master in Britain in 1772 (the year of the Mansfield judgement, which was widely believed to signify the beginning of the end for British slavery). He spent much of the rest of his life writing and campaigning against slavery as a whole, rather than just against the slave trade. One of his campaign letters survives in the Northamptonshire Record Office, addressed to Sir William Dolben of Finedon who introduced legislation in 1788 aimed at improving conditions on board British slave ships. The letter, carefully written in a flowing script, thanks Dolben for his "exertions on behalf of oppressed African countrymen" and comments that the new regulations controlling the number of people carried by each ship "will be the means of saving thousands from the cruel sword of the cursed avarice": the financial greed which he recognised as the root cause of slavery.

Cugoano enclosed a number of anti-slavery tracts with his letter to Dolben. Both Black and White abolitionists were becoming increasingly aware of the need to spread their message throughout the country through writings and public meetings, so as to increase popular pressure upon the decision-makers in Parliament. There is evidence of a sustained letter-writing campaign by a group who sometimes called themselves the "sons of Africa". They included, as well as Cugoano, his friend and colleague Olaudah Equiano. This remarkable man saved enough money to buy his own freedom from slavery in 1766. His adventurous life story, published in 1789, became one of the most influential propaganda weapons of the anti-slavery movement. Like Thomas Clarkson, Equiano travelled the country and probably passed through Northamptonshire many times on his way to Leicester, Nottingham and cities further north.

Olaudah Equiano

The Quakers formed the first British anti-slavery committee in 1783, using their network of local Meetings as a means of rousing opposition. Two years later Equiano wrote to thank them for their efforts; his letter seems to have been valued, for it was copied and circulated. In 1787 Clarkson gathered together a new national committee, linking Anglicans and non-conformists but excluding the Black campaigners from formal membership. The campaign escalated to new levels as Wilberforce's eloquence within Parliament was supported by a deluge of public petitions against slavery. Thousands of men and women began to boycott slave-produced sugar and local anti-slavery societies were formed in many towns. The local and national press carried letters like the one from "An ENGLISHMAN" which appeared in the *Northampton Mercury* in November 1787, describing the cruelty of the slave trade and proclaiming: "For my Part, I had rather be the poor, ignorant, idolatrous Negro, than the Christian merchant or Planter, who dared to treat a Fellow-Creature with such unrelenting brutality."

The American War of Independence helped to stir up the slavery debate without resolving it, and contributed towards the 1787 establishment of a British colony for former slaves in Sierra Leone. The French Revolution had even more mixed results for enslaved people. It opened the way for the greatest slave revolt in history: the Haitian Revolution which, after the defeat of both French and British armies, produced the world's first independent Black Republic in 1805. But in the short run this event stopped the growing British abolition movement in its tracks. The anti-slavery movement seemed unpatriotic and dangerously radical as the overthrow of the French monarchy was followed by years of warfare which threatened Britain itself, as well as the valuable colonies of the Caribbean. It was not until a lull in the fighting that public and parliamentary support once again rallied behind Wilberforce's efforts to end the slave trade. On 25 March 1807 a Bill abolishing the British trade finally passed into law.

The 1807 Abolition Act had multiple causes and was a victory for many different people. But the campaign against slavery was far from over. There were over 750,000 African slaves in the Caribbean and most slave-owners and some British abolitionists expected slavery to continue. It took a fresh wave of slave revolts and another mass campaign in the 1820s and early 1830s to drive home the conclusion that slavery was immoral and dangerous, as well as gradually becoming less profitable and less important to Britain's position as a world power. One of the most famous symbols of the anti-slavery movement was the kneeling figure of a chained slave beseeching "Am I Not a Man and a Brother?". Few of the White abolitionists really believed in the equality of Black and White people, but there was much genuine pity for the slaves' suffering. There was also an increasing tendency for British reformers to identify their own, lesser grievances with the plight of the enslaved Africans.

A new national Anti-Slavery Society was founded in 1823. The conservative William Wilberforce was nearing the end of his parliamentary career, leaving the way clear for more radical leadership by Clarkson and other, younger men. Women, too, began to collect petition signatures and mobilise support for a new sugar boycott, often demanding immediate and total abolition rather than the "gradual" improvements sought by more cautious campaigners. Elizabeth Heyrick, one of the most radical women, lived in Leicester and tracts from the Leicester Auxiliary Anti-Slavery Society found their way to Kettering, and eventually into the collections at the Northamptonshire Record Office. A

John Smith

former slave, Mary Prince, made a moving contribution to anti-slavery propaganda when she published her life history in 1831 with the help of women supporters. Women wielded considerable power as food purchasers and propagandists, though the men were generally reluctant to admit them to their own anti-slavery committees.

Women were also active within the churches and chapels of Northamptonshire, and were deeply stirred by stories of heroic local missionaries caught up in Caribbean slave revolts. John Smith from Rothwell was sent by the London Missionary Society to preach to the slaves in Demerera (now Guyana). Accused of encouraging a major uprising in 1823, he became an anti-slavery martyr when he died in prison after having been tried for sedition and condemned to death by hanging. William Knibb of Kettering travelled to Jamaica in 1824 on behalf of the Baptist Missionary Society. Like John Smith, he insisted upon teaching as well preaching to the slaves, in defiance of the planters' prohibitions. In 1831 Knibb was falsely accused of supporting a much bigger uprising,

William Knibb

led by the Baptist convert Sam Sharpe. Hundreds of people died in mass executions designed to deter future resistance to slavery. Knibb left for England after several weeks in prison, and toured the country campaigning for abolition. It is not surprising to find that soon after Kettering had its own anti-slavery society. Knibb's role is commemorated on Kettering's 1974 coat of arms by a (nowadays widely disliked) image of a semi-naked slave wearing broken shackles.

Kettering coat of arms

The surviving minute book of the Kettering Anti-Slavery Auxiliary Association (1831-35) reveals how the Northamptonshire campaign reached out to the widest possible public. A range of Christian ministers combined with other leading townsmen to form a committee linked to the national society through correspondence, representation at London meetings and mass subscriptions to the *Anti-Slavery Reporter*. Locally, copies of this journal were distributed to "every Book Society in the town". Notices of anti-slavery meetings were "given at the different places of worship" and "200 large Handbills" were printed to be "posted in Kettering and the vicinity". Petition forms were also "sent to the villages in the neighbourhood and recommended to adoption".

Kettering petitioned Parliament not only once, but repeatedly, driving home the demand for immediate and total slavery abolition and condemning "extravagant" compensation for slave-owners. As the anti-slavery campaigners put it in July 1833: "your Petitioners would regard any measure which should fall short of securing to the Slave immediate and entire emancipation, with indignant grief and consternation, and therefore earnestly implore your Honourable House to pass such a measure as shall instantly and absolutely abolish this horrible abomination".

Both in Kettering and in Northampton, the anti-slavery cause became mixed up with local politics. Members of Parliament were required to state their position, and their views on Caribbean slavery were often linked to their opinions on reform issues nearer home. Parliamentary reform, and the prospect of a democratic expansion in the number of voters, was the key issue for many Northamptonians. Election posters from the early 1830s include numerous references to slavery, alongside demands for greater political freedom and economic justice within Britain itself.

By this date the argument among election candidates seems to have been over whether the abolition of slavery should be "gradual" or "immediate", rather than over whether it should happen or not:

> ELECTORS of Northampton.
> Have pity on 800,000 of your fellow Creatures who are in Slavery in our West India Colonies.
> If you return Mr Ross he will only vote for gradual Emancipation
> Remember that for 25 years these gradual emancipators have been deceiving you with fair Promises...if left to them, endless and hopeless Bondage will be the lot of every Slave.
> Northampton, 8th of Dec. 1832.

ELECTORS of Northampton.

HAVE pity on **800,000** of your fellow Creatures who are in Slavery in our West India Colonies.

If you return Mr. ROSS he will only vote for gradual Emancipation, which is the term the West India interest use to deceive you, and to keep the Iniquitous Possession of their unfortunate Slaves.

☞ Remember that for **25 years** these gradual emancipators have been deceiving you with fair Promises, and have done nothing, and if left to them, endless and hopeless Bondage will be the lot of every Slave.

NORTHAMPTON, 8th of DEC. 1832.

Election poster, 1832

The Northampton Quakers, who usually avoided electioneering, published a special poster in support of parliamentary reform, claiming that it would "bring about the speedy and effectual abolition of Negro Slavery". On 31 October 1831 the new Quaker Meeting House in Wellington Street provided the venue for a public lecture by Mr Baldwin of the London Anti-Slavery Society. The *Northampton Mercury* reported that the speaker "appealed affectingly to his hearers, especially to his female hearers – on behalf of the negro...having proved the capability of the negro to participate as fully as the white man in the blessings of civilisation, Mr Baldwin proceeded to show the practicability and safety of abolition".

Despite the advice received from Northamptonshire, the British government decided to end slavery gradually and to allocate £20 million compensation to the planters. The slaves themselves received nothing but their eventual freedom. This was enough to produce

Northampton Quaker Meeting House

heartfelt rejoicing on the Caribbean islands, where, after a four years of compulsory "apprenticeship", 1 August 1838 finally became Emancipation Day. The long campaign against British slavery had ended in a great victory, and at College Street Baptist Chapel in Northampton there were celebrations and a special service. But emancipation was not fully implemented in all places under British rule. It took until 1928 for Britain to extend legal abolition throughout its Empire. Meanwhile the slave trade and slave labour persisted in many other parts of the world. In 1839 the British and Foreign Anti-Slavery Society launched a new global campaign to end slavery, still continuing today under the leadership of Anti-Slavery International.

During the later nineteenth century the most prolonged and extensive anti-slavery campaign was that waged in North America. The British and American campaigns had always been historically linked,

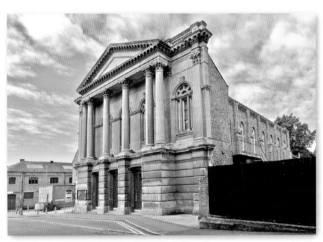

Baptist Chapel, College Street

and this connection made its mark upon the history of Northamptonshire. The third phase of the anti-slavery movement lasted from the British abolition of 1838 until the achievement of American abolition at the end of the American Civil War in 1865. Throughout this period Americans visited Britain to rouse support for their cause. Among them were growing numbers of Black campaigners, often escaped slaves who found sympathetic audiences wherever they travelled.

An 1843 poster printed in Daventry was designed to advertise a series of meetings held by Moses Roper, who had "made his escape from slavery (and has since been pursuing his studies in London)". Audiences were reminded of the "3 million Human Beings" still enslaved in America, and promised the excitement of a personal narrative accompanied by an exhibition of "instruments of torture". Similar instruments found their way to College Street Chapel, brought by a visiting Baptist missionary in 1860 and later deposited at the Northampton Museum.

Clearly the attractions of anti-slavery speakers included their ability to rouse varied emotions. In 1858 George Parnell, "a man of colour and a runaway slave", was lecturing in Market Harborough and Kettering, where the Corn Exchange was "crowded to excess" as he gave "an account of his escape, recapture, and then his escape again, with other particulars of negro life". The lecture lasted for almost two hours, "the last half hour – where he narrated his own personal experience – being the most interesting part". The following year Andrew Jackson, "an American fugitive slave", delivered "a narrative...of his bondage and escape" to audiences in Weedon and Kislingbury, with the support of his wife, "a Creole slave".

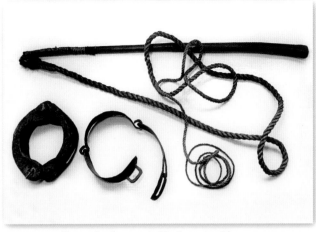

Slavery implements in Northampton Museum

The Northamptonshire public had a longer opportunity to satisfy their curiosity, and their appetite for vicarious excitement laced with moral indignation, when John Anderson arrived in Corby during 1861. Another fugitive, he had made his adventurous way from Louisiana to Canada, where he faced the threat of extradition to answer a murder charge. The Queen's Bench in London decided that a runaway could not be fairly tried for crimes committed during his escape, so Anderson was allowed to remain in Britain. His autobiography, published in 1863, recounts that he was sent away from the distractions of London to study English and mathematics at the British Training Institution in Corby. His fame soon extended throughout Northamptonshire. In November 1861 the *Northampton Mercury* reported that he would support a London anti-slavery speaker at the Northampton Mechanics' Institute, offering the usual account of "the perils attending his escape". It was announced in advance that the lecture's profits would be "devoted to the Emancipation of John Anderson's family, to his education, and to prepare him to be a useful member of society". In 1862 John Anderson was popular enough to be invited as a guest of honour to the Corby Pole Fair. In the same year he was granted land in Liberia and shipped out to Africa, following a farewell banquet and another round of congratulatory and self-congratulatory speeches.

John Anderson

There was more than a hint of condescension in Northamptonshire's welcome to former slaves. The after-glow of the British anti-slavery movement did not last for long, and did not prevent the growth of new forms of racial prejudice as Britain expanded its Empire in Africa and Asia during the second half of the nineteenth century. Northamptonshire had a long history of slave-owning as well as of campaigning against slavery. Both the supporters and opponents of slavery left their mark on the county's history. The slave trade brought Black servants and slaves to Northamptonshire who had not chosen to come here. Yet their descendants sometimes stayed on, married into the local population and became established members of the local community. Slavery abolition was demanded by Black campaigners who freely decided to visit Northamptonshire during the century of anti-slavery struggle, as well as by local writers, reformers and missionaries. As a result of this extended campaign the anti-slavery movement was very widely supported in our county, and played an important long-term role in shaping local attitudes towards the Black presence in British society.

Further Reading:

A. Hochshild, *Bury the Chains. The British Struggle to Abolish Slavery* (London: Pan Books, 2006)
C. Midgley, *Women Against Slavery. The British Campaigns 1780-1870* (London: Routledge, 1992)
R.Reddie, *Abolition! The Struggle to Abolish Slavery in the British Colonies* (Oxford: Lion Hudson, 2007)
D.B. Richardson, *An Indian Preacher in England* (Dartmouth: Dartmouth College MS series 2, 1933)
J. Walvin, *A Short History of Slavery* (London: Penguin Books, 2007)
G.S. Ward, *The 1851 Religious Census of Northamptonshire* (Northampton: Northamptonshire Record Society, 2007)

Websites:
Understanding Slavery; Breaking the Silence; BBC History: Abolition; Encyclopaedia of Slavery; Caribbean Views; National Archives: Abolition of Slavery
The Northamptonshire Black History Association's database gives detailed references to local sources of evidence on Black anti-slavery campaigners: www.northants-black-history.org.uk

Writings of Black Anti-Slavery Campaigners:
Q.O. Cugoano, *Thoughts and Sentiments on the Evil of Slavery, 1787* (London: Penguin, 1999 ed.)
O. Equiano, *The Life of Olaudah Equiano, or Gustavus Vassa the African, 1789* (Harlow: Longman, 1988 ed.)
M. Prince, *The History of Mary Prince, 1831* (London: Penguin, 2000 ed.)
I. Sancho, *The Letters of Ignatius Sancho, 1782* (Edinburgh: Edinburgh University Press, 1994 ed.)

Other Primary Sources:

Northamptonshire Record Office
Dolben (Finedon) collection
Quaker records for Northamptonshire
Anti-slavery pamphlets in Gotch (Kettering) collection
Papers of Kettering Great Meeting (now Toller Church)

Northamptonshire Central Library
Northampton Mercury
Northampton Independent
Minute Book of Kettering Anti-Slavery Auxiliary Association
Dr Culross et al, *History of College Street Chapel, Northampton* (Northampton: Taylor and Son, 1893)

Olney, Buckinghamshire
Cowper and Newton Museum
Olney Parish Church

Kettering
Alfred East Art Gallery and Manor House Museum
Fuller Baptist Church

This chapter was written by Julia Bush

Northamptonshire Workers and the World

While Britain moved towards abolition of the Atlantic slave-trade in 1807 and ending slavery in its colonies nearly thirty years later, what happened to Northamptonshire's Black population? It is not clear whether numbers actually declined in parallel with Britain's diminishing role in the slave trade or whether Black people had simply become integrated in their communities, hidden in a country whose population was expanding and becoming more mobile in an increasingly urban and industrial landscape.

While Northamptonshire did not experience the scale of urbanisation in cities such as Manchester or Leeds, the population of Northampton rose from 11,538 in 1801 to 26,657 in 1851, when three-quarters of its citizens had been born outside the town. Its population then rose rapidly to 87,021 by 1901. That same year 29,000 people lived in Kettering and 18,000 in Wellingborough. For the first half of the nineteenth century at least, this increase was attributed to local migration from rural areas within the county, with more people attracted from further afield by the expanding shoe and leather industry thereafter.

Children on The Mounts in Northampton, 1890s

Black people were certainly present in the county. Some simply passed through, such as the continental traveller Mirza Abu Taleb Khan of Calcutta, who "enjoyed a comfortable supper, and a refreshing sleep, after the fatigue of a long day's journey" in Northampton in January 1801. Others were living in the county. Take, for example, Joseph Louis of Aston Le Walls, "a black from the West Indies Christened and Received in the Congregation of Christ's flock" on 21 November 1804; or James Manuel "A Native of Madagascar Africa" who was baptised in the Parish of Daventry in 1820. However, the changing nature of parish registers, moving from a free-hand style that encouraged a narrative of the event to the use of printed forms that required brevity, may account for the smaller numbers of those we can precisely identify as being Black. The census returns, which are the other major source for studying population in the nineteenth century, identified a place of birth but not ethnicity. From entries in parish registers that do identify Black people, a tentative conclusion might be that they continued to integrate within the local community. William Carter was a Black man living in Towcester. He died in 1807. We know that he had been living in the town for at least twenty years, married a woman named Ann and had three children, Moses, Catherine and Susanna, all of whom died young.

The Carter family were recorded as paupers. For many Black people, when released from service or slavery, everyday life was a struggle for survival on the margins of society, occasionally living on handouts from parish relief and often being moved on. In 1803 Edward Aries, parish constable for

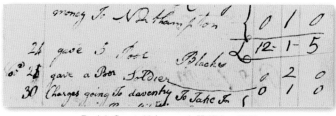

Parish Constable's record, Hellidon 1803

Hellidon "gave 5 Poor Blacks £0 2s.0d". Two years later his successor Jack Edwards gave five shillings once again to "5 Blacks". There are no other records relating to these five people between the two entries and it is likely that they were being helped on their way as they moved through the parish to and from their eventual destination; this job was specific to the parish constable.

Parish officials were keen to avoid liability for the poor other than their own. This is underlined in the Accounts of the Overseers of the Poor for the parish of Finedon, which records "9. Jul. 1806 Gave 3 Black Sailors with a Pass 1s. 0d". Why one might find sailors, let alone Black sailors, in Finedon is not immediately clear, but we do know, for example, that Black slaves were engaged with the Royal Navy, enlisted both as seamen and servants. Once on dry land in England they were left to fend for themselves. A similar group were the lascars – Indian seamen – often pressed into service by the East India Company and left to support themselves and look for employment in ports around the country.

Some Black people turned to radical politics to escape from their condition, such as Robert Wedderburn, an advocate of free speech who was jailed for blasphemous libel in 1819, and William Davidson, who was executed for his part in the Cato Street conspiracy in 1820. William Cuffay was a leading member of the Chartists, the first mass working class movement in Britain. He was accused of planning to start a fire and an uprising, resulting in his transportation to Tasmania in 1848. This was a period of repressive government, using spies and agent provocateurs to root out those they perceived as a threat to the state, and fearful of revolution and unrest as witnessed in mainland Europe as well as on the islands of the Caribbean. Such upheavals could easily be observed by Northamptonshire citizens through provincial newspapers, notably the *Northampton Mercury* and the *Northampton Herald*. The Cato Street conspirators sought to murder members of the government and destroy Parliament, while the Chartists targeted the ballot box. They were disillusioned by the failure of the 1832 electoral reform bill to deliver a fair and full franchise to all men, and drew up a "charter" of demands, including a call for a secret ballot and universal male suffrage (even for most Chartists women's suffrage was a step too far!). Their ideas were ahead of their time and doomed to failure. The *Mercury's* readership would have been well aware of the Chartist movement, the riots and disturbances associated with it, and of course Black people such as Cuffay, who were at the bottom of the political pile. In 1848 it reported on a debate in a Chartist convention led by Cuffay, describing him as "a little, middle-aged, sprightly, and by no means ugly mulatto".

For many other Black people, the reaction to their social condition took a different turn. Where poverty prevailed, crime was just around the corner. At the Northampton Assizes in 1839 "Charles Foundling, a lad of colour pleaded guilty to a charge of stealing three pair of worsted shoes, the property of John Wilson, his master, and was sentenced to One Months Imprisonment". Later records show that this young man was eventually transported to Tasmania as punishment for another theft.

Although Victorians clung to the notion of an identifiable criminal class, in truth most petty crime could be attributed to the struggle to survive. Because criminal records and reports in the local press identify ethnicity, we are able to use these to locate numerous Black people in the county. This is not to say that being Black in the nineteenth century made you more likely to commit crime than anyone else of a similar social standing. We must also place this evidence in the context of changes in policing. There was a general abandonment of private associations for prosecuting felons in favour of an organised police force, and the Northampton Borough and the County Constabularies were created in 1835 and 1840 respectively.

One person well known to the local constabulary was Henry George, a former slave from Tennessee. Obtaining his freedom in 1863, George came to England, married Selina Simon and settled in Northampton in 1890 to raise a family. He became a notable local figure, nicknamed "Black Charley" in a deprived area of the town known as the Boroughs. The harsh reality of life in the Boroughs undoubtedly took its toll and George descended into a life of petty crime and misdemeanour. On the 6 January 1898 the *Northampton Daily Reporter* notified its readers of "Burglaries at Norton and Dodford by a Negro". The report continued: "Henry George (38), a powerfully-built negro, was indicted for burglariously breaking into and entering the dwelling-house of Benjamin Adams, on December 16th, and stealing a bottle of corn cure, a bottle of cordial, a pair of leg straps, and a piece of flannel and needles... He was found guilty of both charges and sentenced to 6 months hard labour for each theft." It was left to the *Wellingborough News* to add: "Mr Batchelor, the prison gate missionary, promised to look after the prisoner at the termination of his sentence, as no doubt his life was a very hard one."

By April the following year even the attentive Mr Batchelor could not prevent Henry George falling foul of the law once more. The *Daily Reporter* again felt obliged to inform the public of an "Affray in College Street" caused by "Henry George, a powerfully built black man, now well known in Northampton", following an incident with Police Sergeant Leatherland. George was sentenced to three months prison with hard labour. Following his release from gaol, George continued to find himself in trouble with his old adversary, Sergeant Leatherland, and was accused of "Serious Assaults on the Northampton Police" after being suspected of stealing a 2d loaf of bread (which he denied). Some time later Henry George secured employment at the Electric Power Station, but died in the workhouse in 1926.

There are numerous other cases involving Black people, some more violent in nature, including Rosa Jarvis "a young negro" aged 20 and Jackson Rivers, a cook aged 33 and described as a "violent negro". Both were well-known in the town, and were charged for violent assault in 1887 and 1896 respectively.

To the association between poverty and crime we might also add drunkenness; certainly this was uppermost in many nineteenth century minds in Northamptonshire as witnessed by the growth of the temperance movement. A poet in the *Northamptonshire Teetotal Friend*, January 1867, was prompted to recite the following lines about "the drink":

> *It's bad when it nerves a man to do*
> *The crime that he's not accustomed to.*
> *It was bad for the culprit who sighs in gaol,*
> *It's bad for his wife – so pale so pale...*

Clearly such exhortations had little effect upon John Abdallah, "A Negro Hawker", who appeared at the Northampton Petty Sessions on Friday 20 July 1860 "charged with being drunk and disturbing the peace in Commercial Street, Northampton"; or upon John Johnson "an apparently well-educated Negro, a boiler-maker of College Street, Northampton", charged for being drunk and disturbing the peace in Gold Street on 23 July 1861. Both men received relatively small fines. In contrast, the unfortunate Samuel Wilson, "a coloured man in trouble", was sentenced to 14 days imprisonment or 18s fine in 1884 for using insulting language with intent to provoke a breach of the peace, having been previously convicted for being drunk and disorderly.

The number of cases of petty crime involving Black people, such as those noted here, is too small to enable us to draw any firm conclusions. We do not know if they were more likely to be convicted (though clearly some denied the charges) or whether Black people were treated differently when they were victims. The value of such records lies in the insights that they offer into the lives of Black

Police photograph, 1896

people in Northamptonshire. For example, we know that John Abdallah was married to an "English woman" named Mary Ann; while Samuel Wilson was a musician aged 62, born in the Unites States of America, who displayed a wonderful array of tattoos on his forearms, including the words "liberty forever". Other criminal records simply enable us to record further Black presence in this period, such as John Williams "a man of colour" in Daventry, charged for being drunk in 1896. A photograph located in the Police Museum, Northampton, shows a Black man wearing a prison uniform, holding up a plate showing the name "Barker" and the date "14.8.96".

Most of the Black people in Northamptonshire during the nineteenth century continued to live their lives in an unobtrusive manner, untouched by central government and most kinds of officialdom, and only rarely do we catch a glimpse of them in the records or artefacts that reflect the rhythm of everyday life. One such record is the school logbook, a diary of events kept by head teachers. An entry in the log book of

Pytchley School logbook, 1869

Isham National School reads: "Jan 27th 1869. Children rather excited on account of the visit of a Negro boy". A week later, it is noted: "A negro enters as scholar". In May 1869, the nearby Pytchley School "Admitted a black boy from Africa" - perhaps the same boy?

Further evidence can be uncovered through memorial inscriptions, as changing attitudes towards death in this period have left us with a greater number of headstones in churchyards. The graves of some earlier Black slaves and servants have been noted in Chapter Three, but one gravestone in particular draws us to a Victorian woman who was much-loved and remembered in her community. The grave of Catherine "Kitty" Prentice is located in the churchyard of Woodford by Thrapston, and it is marked by a stone with the following inscription:

Kitty
After years of faithful & loving service in India and England
fell asleep in Christ XXVII MDCCCLXV (27 May 1865)
not merely a servant but above a servant a sister beloved

According to her burial record, entered on the day following her death, Catherine Prentice was an "African Nurse to Rev GAF Watson Chaplin HMIS aged about 30". George Augustus Frederick Watson became a priest in Bombay, where he also taught, in 1847. From 1851-55 he was curate of Islip, then a Chaplain of the East India Company from 1855-1877. On one of his return journeys he had brought Kitty to Northamptonshire to care for his children.

Kitty's gravestone also serves as a reminder that Britain's fortune was bound up with overseas activities in pursuit of wealth and free trade and, above all, in the rush for empire in competition with the other European powers. Northamptonshire was not remote from the growth of

Catherine Prentice's gravestone

empire as many of its inhabitants found their livelihoods, religious beliefs and other activities interwoven with colonial interests, just as they had been earlier with the slave-trade. This included people employed by organisations such as the East India Company, as well as local missionaries and Northamptonshire businesses that relied on trade with the colonies. Most notable of all was the shoe and leather trade, so important to the economy of the county that by 1870 over 40 per cent of the county's male workforce was employed in the industry. Companies such as the Loake Brothers of Kettering, Moses Manfield and Isaac Campbell & Co. benefited from trade around the world in addition to traditional markets such as those provided by the military. Records of Loake Brothers at the Northamptonshire Records Office include a 1913 agreement to appoint J.S. Brownlee as the company's agent in the Far East.

It was not just the boots carrying armies across continents that were connected to Northamptonshire, but the regiments and soldiers themselves. As early as 1755 the Northamptonshire Regiment had seen service in the colonies in North America and, notably, the West Indies in the 1790s. During the first half of the nineteenth century they were stationed in Ceylon (1828-1839), the West Indies again (1844-1847), Australia and New Zealand (1843-1859) and India (1858-1874). It is not surprising to find numerous Black soldiers attached to the 48th and 58th Foot, Northamptonshire 1st and 2nd Regiment, and it is worth recording their contribution in some detail.

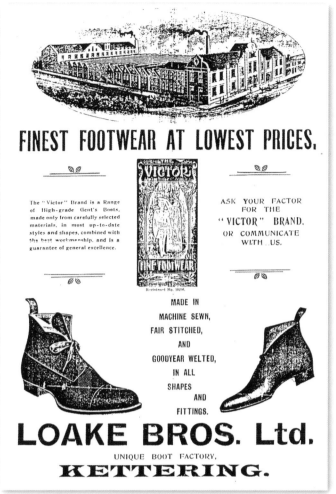

Loake Brothers advertisement

John Billey, born in St Ann's, Barbados, had "black hair, black eyes, a black complexion and was a labourer by trade". He enlisted in the 58th Foot (2nd Northamptonshire Regiment) in Southampton on 6 March 1818 aged fourteen years. Literate and of good character, he saw service in Jamaica and Ceylon. Twenty-one years later he was discharged as a Drummer and provided with a pension. Joseph Bonnie, meanwhile, was born in St Lucia. He is recorded as a "man of colour", and a labourer who served four years as a Drummer in the "Northampton Shire Militia" from April 1798 to April 1802 before joining the Life Guards. Thomas Draper, "a Black foreigner", enlisted in the 58th Rutland Regiment (later the 2nd Northamptonshire Regiment) in 1822 aged twenty-four years.

Black soldiers were not just from the Caribbean. James and William Damerun were Anglo-Indian brothers born in Trinchinoply, East Indies, who served in the 1st Northamptonshire Regiment from 1824 to 1834. They were most likely the sons from a marriage between a white soldier and an Indian woman (such unions were encouraged at this time), and they opted to stay in Asia when their regiment returned home. Consequently they were both transferred to the 58th Foot. However, this is where their similarity seems to end. The discharge papers for James Damerun note that he was prone to vice and bad behaviour, while William was "a good & efficient soldier".

From the 1850s the Northamptonshire Regiment, together with the rest of the British Army, was involved in campaigns to expand the Empire in Asia, Africa and the Pacific, in places such as New

Northamptonshire Regiment drum

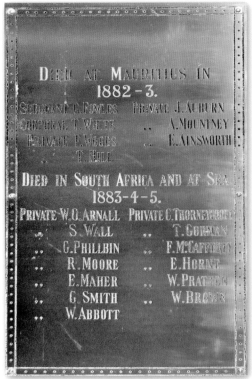

Northamptonshire Regiment memorial,
Holy Sepulchre Church

Zealand, where they helped dispossess the Maoris; Southern Africa, where they fought in the Zulu and Boer Wars, the latter campaign including a volunteer company raised in the county; and again in India. Ordinary soldiers' lives were now bound up in campaigns thousands of miles away from home, where they experienced new landscapes and cultures.

One such soldier was William Cory, born in Milton Malsor, Northamptonshire, and later resident in Far Cotton. He enlisted with the Norfolk Regiment and the notebook he carried with him during his tour of duty has survived. It provides a remarkable insight into the life of a serviceman, containing poems, jokes, songs and recipes, in addition to a narrative of his adventures. His "Jowaki Expedition Song" reflects the first action he saw on the Indian Frontier in 1877. In an upbeat mood he recorded:

> *They quickly took possession of the valley and heights of Bori*
> *And that night they spent right merrily with song and jest and story.*
> *Next morn before the sun they rose with loyal Pathan and Sikh-*
> *They crossed the valley at a run, the Jowaki rogues to meet."*

But in his later poems, Cory appears tired of life in India and Afghanistan. "Oh why did I enlist, a soldier to be", he wrote in a "The Life of a Soldier in India", bemoaning the disease and climate and making many disparaging remarks about the local people, but never questioning and indeed taking comfort from Britain's colonial policy. Some soldiers brought their families with them and some children were born in the colonies. For example, four of the six children of Colour Sergeant John Williams and his wife Kate were born in India.

Extract from William Cory's notebook

Other Northamptonshire people, including Cornwallis Cartwright of Aynho (whose early nineteenth century Indian career is described in Chapter Two), went to the colonies as administrators. In the 1881 census at least 166 people in Northamptonshire gave their place of birth as India. Thus a complex and multi-layered relationship between even a provincial county such as Northamptonshire and the rest of the world was beginning to form.

For the many citizens of Northamptonshire who would never visit Britain's colonies, there were plenty of other opportunities to experience "exotic" cultures. Many artefacts from around the world found their way back to Northamptonshire via the local regiment, such as a shoulder belt in Abington Park Museum, Northampton, which belonged to Hajisheik Jumen, the regimental haircutter, and included a caption engraved in English and Urdu. Other "trophies" imported by Victorian soldiers, businessmen and tourists, serve as a catalogue of conquest. Imperial expansion culminated in the "Scramble for Africa" between European states towards the end of the century, as Britain and its rivals sought raw materials to support industrial growth, a market for its end-produce, and high returns on investment capital, notably by exploiting Africa's mineral wealth (including gold). Northampton Museum's large "ethnographic collection" includes Zulu shields; two Sudanese spears taken at the battle of Omdurman in 1898; an ivory armlet, sickle and dagger from East Africa; a tribal sceptre from Somalia; a stringed musical instrument from Sudan; spears and ceremonial stools from West Africa, and much more.

Zulu shield, Northampton Museum

Ghana stools, Northampton Museum

For some, certain imperial trophies reinforced the racial justification for empire. In 1888 an article in the *Northampton Mercury* described the Hunterian Museum in London, a collection of anatomical specimens, noting that:

> *Among the numerous and valuable curiosities collected by John Hunter [1728-93] and preserved in his Museum there is none greater than his collection of sculls. There is a regular and continued Graduation of these from the most imperfect of the Animal to the most perfect of the Human Species. The most perfect Human Scull is the European, the most imperfect of the species is the Negro. The European, the Negro and the Monkey, form a regular series. Mr Hunter ... facetiously observed, that, in placing the Negro above the monkey, great honour was due to him, for although a Man he could hardly be called a Brother. He also remarked that our first Parents Adam and Eve, were indisputably black...*

In this respect, attitudes toward Black people over the previous hundred years had not advanced at all. In fact, by the late nineteenth century new "scientific" justifications had been developed for racial hierarchy.

A further, though perhaps more benign, justification for British rule was the desire to bring Christianity to Africa and Asia, a result of increasing evangelism in the Anglican and non-conformist churches. Throughout the nineteenth century numerous missionary societies had strengthened their ties around the world. This increased the number of Black visitors to Britain, notably in Northamptonshire, due to its strong links with the Baptist Missionary Society. An early Indian pilgrim sought William Carey's birthplace in 1845 (see Chapter Two). In 1871 the Autumnal Session of the Baptist Union of England and Wales was held in Northampton. Speakers included the Rev Benjamin Millard from Jamaica and the Rev. Goolzar Shah from Calcutta. Other notable visitors arrived in 1892 for the Baptist Missionary

Society centenary celebrations held in Kettering, which led a reporter from the *Northampton Mercury* to remark: "As the morning passed the town became more and more filled up with the arrivals, which included persons of all nationalities, the number of dusky natives being very noticeable."

The centenary was considered to be "a tremendous meeting, the like of which has never before been seen in this part of the county ... probably about 4000". Addresses were delivered by Reverend W. Armstrong, "a native of Burmah", Reverend D. Johnson of East Jamaica and Reverend Joseph Jackson Fuller, a "coloured" Minister from Africa. Joseph Jackson Fuller was born in Jamaica in 1825. He left in 1844 to become one of the first Black Baptist Missionaries in Africa, and the first on Fernando Po Island in the Cameroons. By the 1880s he was living in London with his English wife, Charlotte Diboll. He drew large crowds to meetings around the country, giving lectures on the abolition of slavery in Jamaica and pleading the cause of Africans.

Britain's imperial rule also encouraged people from around the world to migrate to the "Motherland", including inland counties such as Northamptonshire, in search of education and employment. Those who hoped to engage in a profession were especially attracted to Britain. The Victorian medical profession was notable for an increase in the number of Black people entering its ranks. The acclaimed Mary Seacole, though mistrusted by Florence Nightingale, was a pioneer in nursing British troops during the Crimean War, establishing a "British Hotel" between Balaklava and Sevastopol in 1855, in an area where the 48th Foot (1st Northamptonshire Regiment) was also stationed.

Until the mid-nineteenth century the health professions were held in low regard. Indeed, the Medical Register was only created in 1850, followed by the establishment of the General Medical Council in 1858. There was very little opportunity for Black people to study medicine in their homelands and those who aspired to become doctors had to train in Britain (or Ireland and Canada), such as William Davies and James Africanus Horton, both from Sierra Leone. Many others came from Asia. Indian doctors included Kashmiri Mull and Chundra Lall, who are captured in a group photograph in 1897 in front of Obelisk House, Finedon, on the occasion of the ninetieth birthday of Elsie Hawthorne. They were apparently associated with a local physician, Dr. Robb. Interestingly, Dr. Lall's brass plate, inscribed "C.C.Lall., M.B., C.M.(Edin.), Physician & Surgeon", was uncovered in the garden of Kenmure House, Finedon, possibly where he resided and practised medicine. These pioneers were later followed by Dr Bhandari, who served at the temporary Army hospital in Barry Road, Northampton, during the First World War (see Chapter Seven).

By the end of the century it would not have been uncommon for people in Northamptonshire, or indeed Britain as a whole, to come into some sort of contact with people from all parts of the globe. The Black population appeared to be on the increase and amongst many, notably the Black professional classes, an increasing solidarity formed in opposition to colonialism. Some wished for all Black people to come together, culminating in the first Pan-African Conference, which was held in London in 1900. Meanwhile people originating from India campaigned for Indian self-government, including Dadabhai Naoroji, the first Asian to be elected to the House of Commons and a supporter of the Pan-African Conference, and Womesh Chandra Bonnerjee, first president of the Indian National Congress. In 1888 these important leaders were invited to speak at Northampton Town Hall on Indian grievances against British colonial rule by the local radical MP Charles Bradlaugh (see Chapter Two).

On 18 May 1900, when news came through that the siege of Mafeking in South Africa had ended in British victory, thousands of people took to the streets of Northampton. Celebrations continued the following day with the largest procession the town had ever seen, ending in fireworks and a bonfire thirty-six feet high. In some respects this was a realistic acknowledgement of the direct link between Britain's colonial expansion and their own economic well being, rather than simply blind nationalism. However, while some were lighting a bonfire for the Empire, Black people in Britain were beginning to light a beacon for complete emancipation, just as they had done in opposition to slavery one hundred years earlier.

Northamptonshire volunteers for the South Africa War

Further reading:

General:

D. Dabydeen et al (ed.), *The Oxford Companion to Black British History* (Oxford: Oxford University Press, 2007)

P. Fryer, *Staying Power: The History of Black People in Britain* (London: Pluto Press, 1984)

G. Gerzina, (ed.), *Black Victorians/Black Victoriana* (New Jersey: Rutgers University Press, 2003)

Crime:

R. Cowley, *Guilty M'lud!: The criminal history of Northamptonshire* (Kettering: Peg and Whistle Books, 1998)

Military and Empire:

J. Bush, *Moving On, Northamptonshire and the Wider World* (Northampton: Nene Publications, 1989)

J. Ellis, 'Black soldiers in Northamptonshire Regiments of the British Army or the Northamptonshire Militia in the early nineteenth century' (unpublished thesis)

R. Gurney, *History of the Northamptonshire Regiment 1742-1934* (Aldershot: Gale and Polden, 1935)

Religion (Baptists):

Oxford Dictionary of National Biography (Oxford: Oxford University Press, 2004)

Northamptonshire Central Library, Northamptonshire Studies collection, contains numerous primary and secondary sources for the study of the Northamptonshire Association of Baptists and the Baptist Missionary Society, including the lives of Andrew Fuller, John Ryland, John Collett Ryland and William Carey.

Primary sources:

The Northamptonshire Black History Association database will help readers locate numerous primary (and secondary) sources for the study of the Black presence in nineteenth century Northamptonshire: www.northants-black-history.org.uk

Local newspapers, especially the *Northampton Mercury* (from 1720) and the *Northampton Herald* (from 1834) provide a wealth of information.

Parish Records including registers (and transcripts), churchwarden accounts and constables' accounts are available at the Northamptonshire Record Office.

Census returns for Northamptonshire (1841-1901) are available in Northamptonshire Central Library and many are also now available online.

This chapter was written by Terry Bracher

Some Victorian and Edwardian Visitors

Chapter 6

It is as important for us to find out about the rich and famous Black people who are associated with Northamptonshire as it is to find out about local working class people and the very poor. It was not uncommon during the era of servants and slavery for articulate, eloquent Black writers who were not slaves to have their experiences published. This chapter is going to explore distinguished, wealthy, educated Black and Asian visitors to Northamptonshire whose visits were made possible by the Victorian growth of the Empire leading to an increased opportunity for travel across the world. Arriving in Northamptonshire were workers, traders, entertainers, students, politicians, professionals, and royalty, to name but a few. During the period between 1870 and 1920 some very notable people visited Northamptonshire and it is going to be difficult not to talk about them all. However, to do justice, the chapter will only concentrate on a handful of visitors. The information is here to whet your appetite to find out more about these people and others, and to raise some questions which have not yet been fully answered. Why did they visit Britain and what is their connection to Northamptonshire? Do we know more about them because the nineteenth century had more of a taste for local news, as opposed to national and international news? Were there more male visitors than female visitors, or were Black women considered less newsworthy?

The stories that unfold are of extraordinary Black people living in or passing through Northamptonshire. Their lives intermingled and influenced the lives of ordinary Northamptonians and left lasting impressions. Enjoying reading about other people is a popular past-time, and hopefully the following stories will open up other adventurous avenues for exploration.

Royalty: Princess Kaiulani (1875-1899)

This is a tragic story about a young, tall, slim and beautiful Polynesian Princess. Princess Victoria Kaiulani Kalaninuiahilalalapa Kawekiui Lunalilo, born on 16 October 1875, was named after England's Queen Victoria who was a long-time friend of the Hawaiian royalty. Her mother was Princess Miriam Likelike, sister of the late King Kalakana, and her father was Scottish-born Archibald Cleghorn, one time governor of Oahu. When she was thirteen, she met and became friends with the writer Robert Louis Stevenson who was her neighbour. In 1889 when she was in her early teens she was sent to Northamptonshire to further her education and to be groomed for her royal status at Great Harrowden Hall near Wellingborough when the lovely old building was a girl's private boarding school, now a golf club. She also lived for a time at Burton Latimer. The 1891 census for Great Harrowden records that Her Royal Highness was a pupil at Great Harrowden Hall and shows her place of birth as Honolulu, Hawaiian Islands. Although her identity was protected, the beautiful Black girl with sweet and charming mannerisms was well known in Wellingborough. She was befriended by the Neville family whilst she resided in Northamptonshire, to whom she presented a photograph of herself and a riding whip.

Princess Kaiulani

Two years after her arrival she became heiress apparent to the throne in Hawaii. The monarchy in Hawaii fell into troubled times in 1893 when a rebellion led by businessmen with interests in the sugar industry overthrew the monarch and demanded that Hawaii be annexed to the United States. Effectively the Princess was exiled. She eventually returned in 1897 after a period in Europe, and campaigned against the American need to control the sugar and other commercial interests. The American press's racist portrayal of the princess as being a backward, barbarian heathen was instead confronted by an exquisite and stylish royal speaking cultured English. In fact she spoke several different languages and was not at all the average "savage". She was an accomplished painter, musician, expert horsewoman and a graceful swimmer, and was idolised by her people. She consistently refused to encourage overthrowing the Republic and placing herself on the throne, as she preferred to safeguard the peace and prosperity of her people.

On the steamer travelling back, she met Captain P. Bradle Strong, son of an ex-Mayor of New York. Notwithstanding the fact that he was an American whose people had stolen her land, the two fell in love and their betrothal was announced on board the ship the day before they reached Hawaii. Sadly, her return was short-lived and her marriage was not to be. She caught a cold during a rainstorm whilst riding her horse and her life came to an untimely end on 6 March 1899, aged only 23. The *Northampton Mercury, Wellingborough News* and other local newspapers recorded her death with the headline: "Death of the Wellingborough Princess... Yesterday a notable event occurred in this city (Honolulu), a Royal funeral, and probably the last that will ever be witnessed in these islands... it is estimated that 20,000 people attended the funeral". Kaiulani's name is as popular in Hawaii now as it was then, with several buildings and tourist attractions being named after her.

Royalty: Prince Kim Rahal (1890-1912)

This is the tale of another young royal who resided in Northamptonshire and lived life with vigour. Kim Rahal was a Moroccan prince, Pasha Ben Hamid Rahal, son of Hassadi Mohammed and Embaka Zimena and cousin of the Sultan of Morocco, Maulay Ab al Hafid. After being privately educated in both Morocco and Cairo, the Prince decided to travel round the world before coming to Britain to study British life and sports in 1907. He came to live for three to four years with the Reverend E. S. Leverton at Wootton Rectory and was tutored by him. While living in Wootton he became very well known in the county and was generally well-liked. There are many newspaper reports of events that he attended during his stay. Captain R. C. Owen, Governor of Mongalia, North Africa was the Prince's godfather and when Rahal was baptised in private by the Rector Leverton in October 1910 he took on the name of his godfather, thus renouncing his Moroccan name as well as his Muslim faith. The parish register of St George, Wootton, records Kim Rahal's baptism: "Baptised on 25th October 1910, Cecil Edward, of Wootton, gentleman." The name Owen was also assumed as a surname on his adoption by the Captain, and he evidently intended to become a naturalised British subject. It is not clear why he wanted to become a British citizen or give up his religion. One can only speculate that there were not many Muslims around in Northamptonshire, and the new identity was assumed as part of the colonial heritage.

Kim Rahal loved racing, on motorbikes and in cars, and became friends with the like-minded William Rhodes Moorhouse of Spratton (who had a Maori grandmother, and was thus of dual heritage). Kim joined the Grafton hunt, went roller skating, played golf, tennis and even gained a place in the county's Second Eleven cricket team. It is not surprising that he was labelled by a journalist as the "Arab prince with a keen sense of fun!". After Reverend Leverton moved to Cornwall, the Prince continued his studies with

Kim Rahal

Reverend W. P. Pinhey. In 1912, whilst staying with the Reverend Pinhey, Rector of Broughton near Huntingdon, he went out with three friends to test a new car. Sadly, he was killed when the car overturned on a bend. A local newspaper reported: "The accompanying picture gives an idea of the wealth of floral tributes at the funeral of C. E. Owen (Kim Rahal), the touring Moroccan Prince, whose tragic death in a motor accident and funeral was reported in last week's issue". The inscription on his gravestone reads: "In Loving Memory of Cecil Edward Owen (Kim) who died Feb 25th 1912 aged 22 years." Being baptised into the Church of England, he was buried according to Anglican rites. There is no mention of any family or friends from Morocco attending his very British funeral, and that is rather sad as he was buried in his native attire.

Kim Rahal's gravestone

Royalty: Kings Khama, Sebele and Bathoen

Neil Parson's book King Khama, Emperor Joe and the Great White Queen details the visit in 1895 of King Khama and his fellow chiefs Sebele and Bathoen from Bechuanaland (now Botswana) to Britain. They were hoping to gather support against the Chartered Company of South Africa and Cecil Rhodes' plan to take control of their country. They had come to make a direct appeal to the British government and people. The kings were accompanied by an interpreter, and arrived by train in Wellingborough, a manufacturing and market town in Northamptonshire, at midday on Tuesday 24 September. Their host was Mr A. de Sales Turland, a businessman they had met on their travelling ship the Tantallon Castle. The visiting party lunched at the Hind Hotel (still in operation), and then enjoyed an hour and a half tour of Henry Hanger's shoe factory in Kettering. King Khama's first concern upon seeing the huge production was for the number of animals that had died, but he was also impressed by the quickness of the manufacturing process. The three kings attracted great interest from the factory workers and the *Wellingborough Post* reported "nothing formidable in the visitors. They looked like shrewd men... attired in English costume... big and well built."

Khama, Sebele and Bathoen

The kings left the factory with gifts of boots as a memento of their visit. After supper with Mr Turland that evening, they spoke to over five hundred people at Wellingborough Congregational School in Salem Lane. King Khama spoke first, with the aid of an interpreter. He was succinct and to the point: "While we were in Africa, we heard that the Imperial Government were going to hand us over to the chartered Company . . . why. . . .We don't want a new government; we want the old Government. Why should the great Queen throw us from under her own Government?" Similar speeches were made by Sebele and repeated by Bathoen. The speeches were applauded and the views of the speakers were sent to Joseph Chamberlain, the British Colonial Secretary. The *Northampton Mercury* reported on the 27 September: "They aroused much local interest in the three kings' mission and the greatest sympathy has been established on behalf of their cause." Bechuanaland remained a separate British protectorate instead of being absorbed into South Africa, and the three kings' visit played a small part in this decision. I say a small part, but the kings genuinely believed that, as a friend, Britain would not betray them. Not long after this event, in fact only four years later, Britain was fighting a major war for the control of South Africa. Despite their earlier sympathy for the kings, the Northamptonshire public seems to have been fully behind this fresh attempt to put Cecil Rhodes' imperialist vision into action. In 1964 Seretse Khama, the great grandson of King Khama, became the first president of an independent Botswana.

Companions and Guides: James Chuma and Abdullah Susi

This is a legend of Susi and Chuma, the African guides who accompanied Dr David Livingstone on his journeys and exploration of Central Africa. Livingstone was a missionary doctor who first arrived in Africa in 1849. He began to explore uncharted areas of the continent and eventually "discovered" (and named) the Victoria Falls. He was accompanied on his journeys by many African guides who became his friends and companions. Without them, he would have achieved very little. Two of these companions, Susi and Chuma, have an interesting connection to Northamptonshire.

Dr Livingstone fought off ill health on many occasions but in May 1873, despite the attentions of Susi and Chuma, it was evident that he was dying. One night they went into his hut, and by the light of a dim candle they found Livingstone kneeling by his bedside, his head buried in his hands, dead. The faithful companions buried his heart on the spot where he died, Ilala, on Lake Bangweolo, under the shadow of the Myula tree in the still forest, now the site of a Livingstone memorial. Together with Livingstone's other guide Jacob Wainwright, Susi and Chuma embalmed the body before carrying their beloved master for eleven months over hundreds of miles to the coast. They braved hardships, hunger and thirst, until they could give his body into the hands of the English settlers at Zanzibar, from where it was transported back to Britain. Wainwright was allowed to accompany Livingstone's body on the voyage home - only after his passage was funded by the Church Missionary Society - but Chuma and Susi were left behind despite their astonishing devotion to their former master. They were not able to attend his grand funeral in Westminster Abbey.

The following year, in 1874, they finally came to Britain to pay their respects and during their travels they visited and stayed with Reverend Horace Waller of Twywell, near Kettering, Northamptonshire who was writing a biography of Livingstone. Reverend Waller was so disgusted that Susi and Chuma had not been allowed to travel back with Dr Livingstone's body that he wrote a letter to the editor of *The Times* newspaper on 31 March 1874: "They have of late years acted as his head men, they have followed him in all his wanderings and discoveries...is it too much to say that they remain among the greatest African travellers of the present day?...it is a matter of deep regret that when the Abbey vault closes over Africa's benefactor, two of the chiefest mourners will have been shut out from want of a little activity in insuring their presence."

Susi and Chuma with Livingstone's relatives and Horace Waller

Claire Pettitt's book *Dr Livingstone I Presume? Missionaries, Journalists, Explorers and Empires* tells how Susi and Chuma had been invited by Queen Victoria to visit Livingstone's homeland, and were brought over by Livingstone's friend, James Young, the Scotsman who had made his fortune from paraffin. The book also explores the "racist" reactions of Victorian Britain to these visitors. Despite their celebrity status, and their leadership role within Livingstone's exploration, they were made to live and eat with British servants. Pettitt says: "although lauded as emblems of fidelity, loyalty and obedience, they were quartered with other servants on their tour around the country". Susi and Chuma were left feeling uncomfortable and confused by the way they had been treated, one moment as celebrities, then ignored, and they soon returned to Africa.

Henry Stanley of the *New York Herald*, who coined the phrase "Dr Livingstone, I presume?" during his own trip to East Africa in search of Livingstone, reported Susi's "very bad drinking habits" and Chuma's death just eight years later from consumption. The legend of Livingstone is inseparably associated with that of Susi and Chuma: had it not been for their expert guidance, bravery and loyalty, there may not have been as much interest in Livingstone.

Twywell Church memorial carvings

Reverend Horace Waller died in the 1890s. He is commemorated by carved choir stalls in Twywell church which, in their turn, commemorate David Livingstone's opposition to African slavery. The vivid carvings show Arab slave traders and helpless, suffering Africans.

Susi and Chuma received very little recognition until 2007, when the Royal Geographical Society mounted a London exhibition about the "Bombay Africans". Like many others, these young men had been rescued from slavery by the British and transported to India, where they learnt the English which made possible their invaluable service to Dr Livingstone. After Livingstone's death, Susi travelled with Henry Stanley in the Congo, helping to establish the town of Kinshasha. Chuma, who had attended the Free Church of Scotland Mission School in Bombay, worked for the Universities' Mission in Central Africa. Both men received medals from the Royal Geographical Society.

I hope you have had a taste of the rich and famous who are associated with Northamptonshire during the Edwardian and Victorian times. For many of Northamptonshire's visitors, being educated in Britain or by the British was very much sought after and considered an honour, and those that achieved this status were considered very lucky.

They were here for different reasons: some to educate themselves, some to provide a service and some to convince others to visit. Above all, many visitors were passionate and determined people, and although influenced in their own way by the British Empire they also took strength from their racial identity. For example, Princess Kaiulani gained a western education and used her intellect wisely for the benefit of the Hawaiian people, and the three Bechuanaland chiefs helped to prevent their territory from being annexed by Cecil Rhodes and his South Africa Company. Susi and Chuma, who paid their last respects to Dr Livingstone, were not prepared to be treated as second class citizens and returned to their native Africa confused by British hypocrisy. The pride of each one of these individuals shows passion and integrity. I hope this chapter has served to inform you about a part of Northamptonshire's Black heritage which is to be treasured, valued and remembered.

James Chuma

Further Reading:

J. Mebane, *The April of Her Age. Princess Victoria Kaiulani and Robert Louis Stevenson* (Edinburgh: Pentland Press, 1995)

N. Parsons, *King Khama, Emperor Joe and the Great White Queen: Victorian Britain Through African Eyes* (Chicago: University of Chicago Press, 1998)

C. Pettitt, *Dr Livingstone, I Presume? Missionaries, Journalists, Explorers and Empires* (London: Profile Books, 2007)

F. Stanley and D. Stanley, *The Last Princess: The Story of Princess Kaiulani of Hawaii* (New Jersey: Prentice Hall, 1991)

Royal Geographical Society, Bombay Africans online exhibition: www.rgs.org

Primary sources
Northampton Independent
Northampton Mercury
Wellingborough News
Wellingborough Post
Detailed references to the local press reports and other documents used in this chapter can be found on the Northamptonshire Black History Association database: www.northants-black-history.org.uk
See also *The Times* digital archive for national reports.

This chapter was written by Ruchira Leisten

Two World Wars and Local Black History

The two twentieth century World Wars have played a huge part in shaping recent Black British History. British military and naval history over the previous three centuries had been closely linked to empire-building: as we have seen, the Northamptonshire Regiment was formed to fight imperial wars, and progressed around the globe from one imperial trouble spot to the next. But the World Wars, in their different ways, marked the beginning of the end for the British Empire. As Britain and her Allies achieved costly victories in 1918 and 1945, the national debt piled up, international economic advantage was eroded, and colonial independence movements grew in strength.

The countries of the Empire made military and economic contributions towards victory which have been disgracefully neglected in most British histories of the World Wars. But future acceptance of the existing imperial system was by no means guaranteed. Colonised peoples tried to improve their lives by gaining self-government, and also by seeking opportunities for a better life in the "Mother Country" itself. The Second World War marked a decisive turning point, leading to a general decline in Britain's worldwide power. It also marked the beginning of a major growth in migration to Britain by citizens of the Empire and former Empire: the movement which has been humorously described by Jamaican poet Louise Bennett as "colonisation in reverse".

Later chapters of this book will describe the post-war growth of Black communities in Northamptonshire. The present chapter concentrates on the war years, and the short-term consequences of the two World Wars for local and national history.

The First World War, 1914-18

How did the First World War influence the history of Northamptonshire? Before turning to evidence of its influence upon local Black history, it is important to understand the overall importance of the Empire to the British war effort. Few British history books highlight the fact that almost one third of the troops who fought in the First World War were from the countries of the Empire, rather than from the British Isles. More than 1.4 million men came from India, as volunteers rather than conscripts; this total omits thousands more who performed vital war service in the merchant marine. Indian soldiers were rushed to France in September 1914 to help shore up British and French resistance to the German advance on the Western Front. They later served at Gallipoli, in the Middle East and in East Africa. Over 64,000 lost their lives, and more than 12,000 received bravery awards, including twelve Victoria Crosses.

The racial prejudice of the British War Office placed some restrictions upon Indian soldiers, for example upon their promotion opportunities and conditions of service. But the wartime contribution of Black soldiers of African descent was even more severely controlled, and only slowly expanded as the numbers of dead and wounded mounted and manpower shortages became acute. The two mainly Black battalions of the West India Regiment were at first restricted to labouring duties behind the lines on the Western Front, but later fought bravely alongside other Africans (such as the West African Frontier Force and the King's African Rifles) on more distant battle fronts. In 1915 the British government responded to growing pressure from Caribbean volunteers by forming a new British West Indies Regiment, a separate Black unit which had lower pay and promotion prospects than other regiments and was again mainly restricted to non-combatant duties. Despite this blatant discrimination, soldiers from Africa and the Caribbean eventually won their share of battle honours and suffered their share of casualties. African seamen, like the Indian lascars, remained uncounted despite their importance to the war effort.

Meanwhile men and women of Indian and African descent were also beginning to find their way in small numbers into the regiments recruited within Britain itself. The history of the Black presence in the British Army remains under-researched, but it seems clear that there was much inconsistency of policy towards Black volunteers, whether they were from the colonies or long-term British residents. Official policy discriminated against Black soldiers throughout the war. It was not until June 1918 that the Army Council formally declared that "British subjects of colour may be enlisted into combatant or other units of the British Army"; policy towards Black officers remained negative to the end. This did not prevent some Black people from enlisting earlier, and even (as we shall see) occasionally achieving promotion to officer rank. Opportunities for Black civilian employment also improved during the war, as the war economy expanded and conscription reduced the available workforce.

By the end of the First World War Britain's Black population had grown significantly, though it remained small. 1919 saw a number of ugly incidents, including large-scale riots at British sea-ports, as groups of demobilised White soldiers asserted their resentment of visible minorities. However the surviving evidence from Northamptonshire suggests that the war played some role in broadening British attitudes as well as in increasing the Black presence in the county. Among the county's military recruits was William Rhodes Moorhouse, a daring and wealthy young pilot of Maori descent who had enjoyed hell-raising in Northamptonshire alongside his good friend Kim Rahal during the decade before the war. His death during 1915 was widely mourned. Moorhouse received a posthumous Victoria Cross after he flew on towards his target in France despite enemy attack and slight injury, and successfully unloaded his bombs. By now fatally injured, he returned his aircraft to base and died the next day.

William Rhodes Moorhouse on Northampton Racecourse, 1911

Among the colonial troops who visited Northamptonshire in the course of their service was a group of soldiers from Ceylon (Sri Lanka). Their visit in January 1916 followed the traumatic experience of being rescued from a torpedoed ship. Billeted in St James, Northampton, the troops found themselves generally welcomed. The *Northampton Daily Echo* pointed out that they had "voluntarily travelled thousands of miles, mostly paying their own expenses" in order to defend their "Motherland". Interviewed for the newspaper, the men expressed their liking for their new surroundings in good English. This was more than merely routine politeness, for on 29 July 1916 the *Northampton Independent* quoted a letter received from Private Wijayasingha, now in France and looking back fondly on his stay: "We, the batch of the Cinghalese boys of the torpedoed 'Continent'...wish, through the Independent, to thank the public of Northampton, especially those at St James, for the great kindness shown us which was much appreciated." Mrs Morris of Marlborough Road, St James, had "often entertained Wijaysingha and his comrades", and was now regularly posting the local newspaper out to her new friends.

Another popular man from the Indian subcontinent was Dr Ram Nath Bhandari, who spent the war years serving as Medical Officer at the Barry Road Hospital in Northampton. In September 1919 the *Independent* reported that he was due to sail back to India the next day, after a total of eight years' study and service in Britain. Dr Bhandari was "one of the youngest students who has gained

Dr Bhandari at Barry Road Hospital

the distinction of Doctor of Medicine... his sojourn in this country has made him so attached to the English that he tells me he is sincerely sorry to leave". His qualifications had been awarded by St Andrew's University, where he completed a thesis on the effects of mustard gas upon soldiers in the trenches.

Dr Bhandari was apparently considering a possible return to Britain at a later date. Evidence survives of other men whose temporary visits gradually became permanent, among them Abdul Salem of the Bengal Lancers. After signing up as a drummer boy in Calcutta at the age of fourteen, Abdul found himself travelling the world in support of the British war effort. At the end of the war he re-enlisted in the Cheshire Regiment, rather than returning to India. By the early 1920s he was settled in Northampton with a local wife and a growing family. Known locally as "Darkie Joe", he fathered a son who joined the Army and a daughter who volunteered for the Land Army at the outbreak of the Second World War twenty years later.

Undoubtedly the most popular of Northamptonshire's Black soldiers was Walter Tull, a midfield player for Northampton Town Football Club from 1911-14. This son of a Barbadian father and a Kentish mother had succeeded in becoming a professional footballer after a difficult childhood which included a spell in an orphanage. As only the second Black professional footballer, and the first to play in such a prominent position, he suffered racist abuse from away fans during a short spell at Tottenham

Abdul Salem, 1926

Hotspur. This experience probably made him doubly determined to prove himself, both as a footballer and as a soldier. After volunteering in December 1914 – the first Cobblers player to do so – Tull soon found himself in the thick of the action on the Western Front. Despite injuries and illness, he distinguished himself sufficiently to merit the very unusual honour (for a Black man) of being trained and commissioned as a British Army officer.

By early 1917 Walter Tull was a Second Lieutenant in the 23rd (2nd Football) Battalion of the Middlesex Regiment. A year later the *Northampton Independent* joined his "many friends" in "hearty congratulations" upon a published tribute from his commanding officer, who wrote: "I wish to place on record my appreciation of your gallantry and coolness." During the final

Walter Tull and his brother

months of the war Lieutenant Tull was back in France, fighting in the second battle of the Somme. On 25 March 1918 he was shot through the head and killed while leading an attack. His men struggled to bring his body back for burial, but were forced to abandon him in no-man's-land. His name was eventually placed on the wall at the Arras memorial, but he has no marked grave. Though he was born in Britain and lived all his life in this country, he appears in the Commonwealth rather than the British list of the war dead. There was no memorial to him in Northampton till 1999, when a marble tablet was erected outside the football ground, stating: "Through his actions W.D.J.Tull ridiculed the barriers of ignorance that tried to deny people of colour equality with their contemporaries. His life stands testament to a determination to confront those people and those obstacles that sought to diminish him and the World in which he lived."

Walter Tull memorial

The Second World War, 1939-45

Northamptonshire's contributions to both World Wars are annually commemorated at Remembrance Day ceremonies all over the county. At the heart of these ceremonies are the men who died, and whose names are tragically listed on local war memorials. The wounded and the families of those who suffered are also remembered, and the victims of later wars usually find due mention. However colonial troops and colonial seamen have received belated and inadequate recognition in this country. The Hyde Park memorial gate for colonial war service was dedicated as recently as 2001. Perhaps it is not surprising to find that some local Black people whose friends and relatives contributed to the Second World War feel excluded from the annual British act of remembrance. As we move into the history of more recent times, the oral history archive of the Northamptonshire Black History Association becomes an important new source of evidence, alongside photographic and printed records. It begins to tell us how people felt during and after the war, as well as how they acted.

To begin once again with the statistics: India contributed more than 2.5 million men to the Indian Army, despite the fact that the Second World War coincided with the nationalist Congress Party's call upon the British government to "Quit India". They bore much of the burden of the campaigns in the Far East. At the same time 372,000 men from Britain's African colonies served in Burma and the Middle East as well as in Africa itself. Hundreds enlisted into a new Caribbean Regiment, which served in Egypt and Italy as well as the Caribbean. Thousands of West Indians volunteered for service in Britain, including three hundred who successfully joined the elite British air crews, and around six thousand (mainly Jamaicans) who entered the Royal Air Force as ground crew. Government policy on Black recruitment to the British forces was more welcoming than during the previous war, but there were still plenty of obstacles to prevent ambitious young men and women from seeking promotion. Colonial soldiers continued to serve for substantially less pay throughout the war, as well as having fewer opportunities to take up leadership roles. Black British soldiers, including those from Africa and the Caribbean, often found themselves caught in the backwash of American military racism.

Finally, it should not be forgotten that civilians as well as servicemen helped to win the war, both in Britain and overseas. In Northamptonshire thousands of civilians provided the boots which shod the Army around the world. In India an enormous textile industry supplied Army uniforms, while other colonial countries provided the raw materials which were essential to the war effort. The Merchant Marine which brought food and other goods to Britain suffered more than 30 per cent casualties among its fifteen thousand colonial seamen. The financial contribution made by the Empire to British victory is still harder to quantify: historians have calculated that Britain owed £450 million to the colonies for colonial produce at the end of the war, while millions more had been raised from poor countries through gifts and interest-free loans. Some colonial workers had also contributed through their war-time labour in British factories and warehouses, though the British trade unions tried hard to defend their absent members' wages against the threat of cheap colonial labour.

Oral history interviews and other surviving evidence illustrate all these different kinds of war service and show how they became woven into the fabric of local history. Local people who grew up in India or in the Caribbean recall the economic disruptions and opportunities of wartime. Still more vividly, they remember the departure of friends and family members for service overseas, sometimes never to return. Winston Nelson's cousin was among the elite air crew recruited from Jamaica: "He didn't live long. He was a tail gunner and they shot off the rear of the plane so he died quite early." For Saeed Ahmed Pirzada, growing up in India during the war, memories centre around his family's loss of trained servants, lured away by the false promises of profiteering agents. He remembers food rationing and shortages of "all the basic necessities" as supplies were redirected to the troops, and the suffering of families whose youngsters were "taken away to serve in the Army...when they came back they had difficulties in adjusting and similarly lots of people didn't even return and their families – naturally, they had hard times." Looking back with sadness, he feels that "It wasn't our war".

Albert Salem

Abdul Salem's son Albert, born and raised in Northampton, recorded some more cheerful experiences. During the war he acted as a tank instructor for the Eighth Army, and eventually returned safely home. A talented artist and footballer before the war, Albert kept in touch with Northampton by sending back cartoons of his war service for the *Chronicle and Echo*, including this one illustrating British soldiers' rescue of local ladies during the Italian campaign. His younger brother remembers war-time "leave" visits celebrated by the purchase of lead soldiers in the Market Square. Albert was just one out of thousands of Northamptonshire men who found themselves serving long periods overseas. The local regiment saw action in most of the main theatres of war, suffering heavy casualties and winning high honours.

The number of surviving ex-servicemen from World War II is now declining steeply, but recorded life histories at the Northamptonshire Record Office include those of

Albert Salem's cartoon

Black soldiers, sailors and airmen. As in the First World War, colonial recruits were all volunteers. They included seventeen year-old Winston Nelson, who lived up to his name by volunteering for the Royal Navy Volunteer Reserve in 1942, and joining the crew of a minesweeper active in the defence of the Caribbean against German submarines. Two years later both Winston Nelson and George Cleghorn volunteered for the Royal Air Force, and for service in Britain itself. A clever young man from a farming family, George Cleghorn had hopes of training as a mechanic, and dreamt of eventually flying a plane, as well as of helping to defeat Britain's enemies: "We came to defend the Mother Country and our country, just the same." After their arrival at chilly British bases, a few weeks of basic military training ("square-bashing") was followed by unglamorous months of "General duties. Like loading things on the lorries for war service, making tea, delivering mails, keeping the yard clean, picking up papers, and everything you could think of." Increased knowledge of the war brought greater understanding of its dangers, and a growing dread of being posted to Burma: "that was the war that was really the most frightening".

George Cleghorn in RAF uniform

In the meantime there were the consolations of serving a common purpose, and of friendly company both inside and outside the base: "You'd meet a man, you didn't know him, or a woman soldier called a WRN or ATS, which is a soldier woman, and you'd share a cigarette just like that. Travelling in the train, you'd just make friends with them because you are fighting for the one cause." Local civilians were part of the same friendly circle, especially when the Jamaican airmen shared their own more generous rations: "the average citizen would look to you to give him a bit of chocolate or a cigarette...of course you treat the natives, you have a pint of beer and a cigarette and you all sit there and enjoy yourselves, you know, you have a singing competition and things like that. We were popular at that time, yes." The end of the war brought tremendous rejoicing and "a jolly good dance of course that night, to make a celebration...We were very happy and relieved that we were still not dead! We didn't have to go to Burma." Like most others, George Cleghorn hurried back to Jamaica and used his government compensation to buy a plot of land. It was not until fourteen years later that he decided to return to Britain, once again hoping for better opportunities and expecting a friendly reception from the country he had served.

Lilian Bader in WAAF uniform

Women soldiers in the Second World War included small numbers from the Caribbean who had to overcome racial as well as gender prejudice from the Army and the British government before being allowed to play their part. Women born in this country sometimes did not find things much easier. Lilian Bader was the daughter of a Jamaican father and an English mother. After a short spell in a military canteen (from which she was strangely dismissed on the grounds that her father was not born in Britain), she was eventually accepted into the Women's Auxiliary Air Force in March 1941. Her ability and enthusiasm paid off when she qualified as an instrument repairer, responsible for checking that aircraft instruments were in full working order before each attack. Later she became an Acting Corporal, proudly wearing her stripes at a special dining table set aside for non-commissioned officers. Her husband, Ramsay Bader, eventually brought her to his foster family's home in Northamptonshire, and she began to raise her own family at the end of the war. Ramsay's father, who was from Sierra Leone, had served

in the First World War and his older brother fought in Burma. Lilian Bader lost one of her brothers on military service, while the other was eventually invalided out of the Merchant Navy.

George Cleghorn and Issim Ullah by Northampton war memorial

Northamptonshire's war veterans include seamen as well as those who served in the armed forces. Issim Ullah, who lived for thirty years in Northampton before his death in 2001, belonged to a long line of Bengali sailors who had been serving the British Empire since the early days of the East India Company. Born in 1913, he signed on for his first voyage from Calcutta at the age of fourteen. Conditions were hard for a stoker aboard British steamers, so on his first trip to London in 1937 Issim "jumped" ship and stayed to watch the coronation of King George V. A meagre living could be made among East London's Bengali community, but when war broke out: "Every morning or evening the police came to say 'Go in the Merchant Navy'. They wouldn't let you stay in London." A succession of highly dangerous voyages followed. On one occasion his ship was torpedoed off Gibraltar, and he was lucky to escape with merely the loss of a finger. After travelling all over the world, he returned thankfully to Bengal at the end of the war, only to find that working his small farm was a still harder way to make a living. By 1953 he was back on board ship, and

eventually found himself stoking British hospital boilers rather than steamships. His family joined him in Northampton, where he founded one of the first Indian restaurants.

American Soldiers in Kettering

The largest wartime increase in Britain's Black population came from the short-term presence of over 100,000 Black American soldiers in the country. The "Black G.I.s" ("General Issue"), like the Jamaican RAF men, were popular with the locals. But their presence brought problems, linked to the racist segregation practices of the American Army. Disciplined by White officers and the White Military Police, the G.I.s were quartered separately and expected to socialise separately when off duty. The British government was reluctant to antagonise Black colonial troops, but still more anxious to appease its American ally. Arrangements were generally made to replicate segregation on British soil, and the Black Americans based in Northamptonshire were directed to Wellingborough's Victoria Centre for their entertainment, rather than to Northampton's pubs and clubs.

Local newspaper reports abound of the friendly reception given to the Black American troops as they paraded local towns, contributed their singing to church services and concerts, and occasionally distinguished themselves by acts of individual bravery during bombing raids. But the less positive side of their presence is reflected in Winston Nelson's memories of being turned away on racial grounds in various parts of the country: "we used to go to a club in Preston. The Americans think like they owned it. We wouldn't tolerate it so we – we wasn't afraid to use our fist. And the Fire Brigade Station was pretty near and they used to back us. They used to turn on the hose and water the Americans!" The American Club in Northampton's Drapery was no more welcoming to Black servicemen: "I've been in there a few times but I didn't go in there much after that because I was on me own...I was outnumbered too much." After the end of the war a curious incident took place in a pub in nearby Sheep Street. Gerald Maloney, son of the well-known Black boxer Jimmy Maloney, was trying to restore order during

American soldiers in Great Doddington

a pub brawl, only to be seized by the American Military Police and hauled off to imprisonment at a neighbouring US base. When his identity was finally proved, "they hushed up the incident...to try and avoid a scandal".

Black American soldiers left another legacy in Northamptonshire, through their relationships with local white women. Sometimes Black babies were unacknowledged by their fathers; but even when a marriage took place and an American father did his best to create a long-term future of family life between two continents, his children were often cruelly labelled as "war remnants". These children included a number of individuals who have gone on to make outstanding contributions to Northamptonshire life.

Second World War victory depended heavily upon the military service of Black men and women, and upon the many other resources which had been mobilised by the Black populations of the British Empire. Yet Britain's gratitude for their sacrifice remains muted. Each year a few members of Northamptonshire's Black communities attend Remembrance Day ceremonies, or the commemorative church service of the West Indian Ex-Servicemen's Association in Clapham, London. A much wider recognition and commemoration is surely overdue, both locally and nationally, from the British government and the British people. A response is needed to the Northamptonshire elders who say:

"I do not support Poppy Day here coz as far as I'm concerned the people who went to the war, all what's going on now, they've never been considered. I mean there's been lots of war show like Armistice Day and things like that and West Indies is never represented, it's never been mentioned. And when you start to think of how many people came over here and die for it and to think, well, they've never been mentioned as if they didn't count." (May Green)

"That's a lot of Black people who come to fight for Mother Country as they call it, never went back... even these Poppy Days when they have it...you never see any Black people walking, but there was a lot of Black people in the World War One and World War Two both, but they're not mentioned. But they were there, they were there." (Monica Noel)

"They're not being recognised although they participated, they joined the war, they fought the war, they were right in the front and they lost their near and dear ones. But they are not remembered as much as (others) who took part in the war and that makes them again bitter and then they feel that, you know, they just participated in that war in vain. That's how they're feeling, yes." (Saeed Ahmed Pirzada)

George Cleghorn commemorating VE Day in 1995

Further reading:

B. Bousquet and C. Douglas, *West Indian Women at War. British racism in World War II* (London: Lawrence and Wishart, 1991)

P. Fryer, *Staying Power. The History of Black People in Britain* (London: Pluto Press, 1984)

C. Holmes, *John Bull's Island. Immigration and British Society, 1871-1971* (London: Macmillan, 1988)

R. Lotz and I. Pegg (eds.), *Under the Imperial Carpet. Essays in Black British History 1780-1950* (Crawley: Rabbit Press, 1986)

M. Phillips and T. Phillips, *Windrush. the Irresistible Rise of Multi-Racial Britain* (London: Harper Collins, 1999)

M. Sherwood and M. Spafford, *Whose Freedom were Africans, Caribbeans and Indians defending in World War II?* (London: Savannah Press, 2000)

R. Visram, *Indians in Britain* (London: Batsford, 1987)

R. Visram, *Asians in Britain. 400 Years of History* (London: Pluto Press, 2002)

R. Winder, *Bloody Foreigners. The Story of Immigration to Britain* (London: Little, Brown, 2004)

Websites

The Imperial War Museum's website includes information about the contribution of Black and Asian soldiers, sailors and airmen during the two World Wars: www.iwm.org.uk

Primary sources:

Detailed local references can be found on the Northamptonshire Black History Association's database: www.northants-black-history.org.uk

The interviews quoted in this chapter are in the Northamptonshire Black History Project's oral history archive, at the Northamptonshire Record Office.

This chapter was written by Julia Bush

The Windrush Generation and After

The Empire Windrush docked at Tilbury on 22 June 1948. This event became symbolically linked with the start of the mass migration from the Caribbean. Black people had already been coming to Britain for hundreds of years, both as visitors and settlers. When Britain set about conquering the high seas and setting up an empire, stronger trade links were gradually made with Africa and African colonies created. Moreover Caribbean colonies were populated with African people by European traders who brought enslaved people from Africa to work on the sugar plantations. After the early nineteenth century abolition of the British slave trade and slavery emancipation in the British colonies, the authorities set about instilling a sense of Britishness in the colonials. The Windrush wave of migration from 1948 to the 1960s is considered unique because of its scale and the impact that it had on the social and cultural landscape of Britain. This wave of immigrants, numbering over 150,000 by 1960, later became the dubbed the Windrush Generation. Some travelled directly to Northamptonshire, to join relatives or search for work. Many arrived in Northamptonshire after living in other areas such as London, Yorkshire or the West Midlands.

Remembering the Windrush arrival at WACA, 1998

After the Second World War the economy in the Caribbean was stagnant, while Britain was short of labour to undertake urgent tasks of economic and social reconstruction. The British colonies had come to the aid of Britain, the Mother Country, to help win the war. Spurred on by a sense of adventure and a desire to improve their lives, 498 passengers boarded the former German troop carrier named the MV Empire Windrush, taking a step into the unknown. Many of these passengers were ex-servicemen who had visited Britain under different circumstances. As the ship sailed to British shores, government officials expressed private concern over an unsolicited "influx" of jobless, homeless Black immigrants. A Colonial Office spokesman was sent to welcome the new arrivals, and at the same time warn them that "Things will not be too easy".

The West Indians, as they were then generally known, were British citizens. They had as much right to live in Britain as the native islanders, due to the Nationality Act of 1948 which gave citizens of the colonies equal rights with native Britons. The populace as whole were at best bemused by the new arrivals, and at worst outright hostile. As time went on the authorities realised that these new arrivals could successfully fill the labour gap and started advertising jobs in Caribbean newspapers. The new National Health Service and London Transport were among the keenest employers, advertising extensively in Jamaica, Barbados and Trinidad. Numbers arriving from the Caribbean closely reflected the fluctuating supply of employment, but eventually the British government responded to political pressure for official controls over immigration. The 1962 Commonwealth Immigrants Act introduced a system of employment vouchers to make it harder for people to come over. This chapter describes the experiences of the Windrush Generation as they made their way in Northamptonshire. It is based on existing publications and local oral history testimony collected by the Northamptonshire Black History Project.

Early experiences of life in Britain were a sharp contrast with life in the Caribbean, which was characterised by close-knit communities, strict schooling, and agricultural and rural settings differing starkly from British urban sprawl. Ray Campbell remembered: "I have fond memories of my childhood...I used to run to school. School was about four or five miles way from where I lived. Close relationships, you know people sort of friendly, very neighbourly, safe environment to live and play but acknowledging that we were very poor but happy."

Many of the arrivals came from relatively well-off backgrounds and some were very well educated. The historian Peter Fryer says that the Windrush Generation of migrants experienced three disappointments. The British populace wrongly believed that migrants from the West Indies were unskilled workers, whereas in fact 46 per cent of the men and 27 per cent of the women were skilled manual workers. A quarter of the men and over half the women were non-manual workers: "Yet the newcomers found themselves in most cases having to settle for a lower job status than they had enjoyed at home." The second disappointment was the difference between the imperialist ideal about Britain that they were taught in school and the cold, mundane reality. The arrivals regarded themselves not as strangers but as Englishmen. The third relates to the cold reception they received here. In 1960 more than two-thirds of the British population held a low opinion of Black people or disapproved of them. A third strongly resisted the idea of Black people living and working in Britain.

The book *Cold Arrival*, published by the Northampton African and Caribbean Elders Society in 1998, collected together testimony of elders from the Caribbean islands alongside background information about the islands. It includes detailed descriptions of the first impressions that the Windrush migrants had of Britain and their struggles, disappointments and successes. The introduction describes the experience of arriving in the Mother Country: "Many Caribbean people had hoped when emigrating to Britain from their respective islands that they would have found ready acceptance for themselves and their children in the 'Mother Country'. They had been nurtured to see in British Society, the Guardians of Rule and Law, the Custodians of Justice and above all a Christian Society, built on tolerance and charity to strangers. The majority did not expect to find a society hostile to Blacks and one in which racial discrimination would be prevalent."

Most of the new arrivals had received a British colonial education and were fully conversant with English literature and history. They were surprised by British people's ignorance, not just of the Caribbean islands as British colonies but also of their own culture. Merlynne Francique explained her surprise and dismay: "When you lived in the Caribbean you have a totally different impression of Britain and you felt that most of the people were educated people and so on... I knew all about Browning and Shakespeare and so on and expected when I spoke to somebody that person would have the same knowledge, level of knowledge and education, and it wasn't the case, so that shocked me."

Ulric Gravesande, Mayor of Northampton

Early arrivals found themselves the object of curiosity. Ulric Gravesande arrived in Northampton in 1957. He describes the curiosity he encountered: "People were friendly in one way... There weren't many of us Black folk around at that time and I don't think many people at that time had the experience of meeting and mixing closely with Black people. So that I had to put up with things like people would want to touch my hair."

Others faced outright hostility and were surprised by the mismatch between the idealised image of Britain that they had been trained in and the unpleasant reality. Bert Cuff remembered: "I suppose what surprised me even more was the people, how different they were in attitude to the ones, to the White people I met in Jamaica...I had a teacher from England who told me how wonderful England was and how people were welcome. That view soon changed once I was here."

The cool welcome was no less of a surprise than the cold weather, for which the arrivals were often unprepared. New arrivals had to get to grips with snow and ice as well as strange buildings and enclosed spaces. Carl McFarlane looked back on his first impressions of England on arrival: "My first thought was God, I didn't know there were so many factories in England. Because all the houses the chimneys, you know I thought every one was a factory...apart from that it was very cold. I've never experience any cold like that."

Cynthia Dyer expressed her shock at the cold and the primitive facilities: "Snow was high on the ground...well, I need the toilet and I said, 'Oh you know, can you show me where it is?' and it was a little shed at the bottom of the yard and I thought, 'Oh no! I didn't know this things [sic] is happening in England.'"

For Sylvia Bowmer, too, the shock of the cold weather was intense. She recalled, "Life was very, very rough and you take the whole lot of time to get in the real system of it...people get very ill because you didn't know how to clothe yourself, to go out to prepare for the winter." Journeys to and from work were a nightmare of frozen feet, steamed-up buses and chilblains: "when you come from work and go to your door...you can hardly turn the key in the door, your finger can't hardly hold the key it was so cold."

The primary aim for most people was to find employment: many had high expectations and hoped to make their fortunes. George Cleghorn arrived in Northampton in 1960: "No, it was not easy...one of the reason why we got a job, reasonable job (was) coz certain White people, White men they didn't want to work, to do a certain type of job, too cheap for them or dirty whatsoever...but because we want a job...we have to take any dirty job to work so as to get the money."

Work was often menial with little chance of advancement. June White Gulley said: "My Dad came to Northampton coz when he went up North somebody said to him 'you want to come to Northampton coz Northampton's a shoe town'. So he thought that he could come here, take off, take over from where he was in Jamaica. And get a shop, maybe have a factory. He didn't realise that Black people weren't invited to come and open stores, they came to do some work what, you know, people didn't really want to do, like work on the buses, work on the railways, and in the factories."

Joe Dixon

The low levels of opportunity were not the only challenge that Black people faced in employment. There are many examples of racist discrimination from colleagues and management. Joe Dixon described his experience: "I applied for work on the

Corporation. I will be frank with you here. I think they were prejudice then, because, when I went there in 1960 I took the test. It was only simple...I passed the test. But the Manager...he said 'at the moment, umm, they hadn't got any vacancies.' And I found out that wasn't true."

Norma McFarlane was fortunate and found an employer who wished to develop her abilities. She started work in a clothes factory and was promoted and offered training, but decided to train instead as a nurse. This experience in a first British job was quite unusual.

More common was the sense of disillusionment when people arrived in Britain and were forced to take low-paid jobs. May Green explained that there was a sense of bitterness about being lied to, as hopes of earning money to improve the family business and return home were dashed: "They wanted people from the West Indies to come and do these jobs because the people here weren't doing it, so we came over. Well they tell you, they advertise it in the paper, then you hear over the radio...what is happening in England and how you could get on with it. I mean the wages were only five pound a week at the time but they never complained, they never mentioned wages."

Another challenge was finding somewhere to live. In the 1950s it was difficult to find landlords who would take Black people. Monica Noel explained what it was like for the first arrivals: "When my Dad first came to England it was like, it was very difficult...because the people won't let, the White people won't give them any houses to rent and who used to rent houses for them, like, it was the Irish people, so if the Irish would give them a room, one man a room... So what the men did was, they used to work in shifts and used the one room, used to be used by about three or four, say six men."

Over-crowding and lack of facilities was a real problem. Janet Douglas-Hall arrived in Britain in 1955: "My mother was, she said, 'You have actually brought me to this country to live like this!'. We lived in a house you know, I've never shared a room with anybody you know, you have your little house there you know, and normal, and here we are sharing a room. And you had to do everything in this room, you had to sleep, cook, eat, everything in this one room and the rent was enormous."

Over time people found ways to save. One method was to set up a 'partner' scheme also known as 'Pardner' or 'Sous-Sous'. Individuals would contribute a sum, for example £5 a week, to a large group and then they would take it in turns to draw the total. This made it possible to make a payment towards a house. As communities settled, they started to buy property. In the Fifties and Sixties Black people experienced discrimination in the housing market as people were not keen to have them as neighbours. Ulric Gravesande talked about his experience buying a house in Northampton: "I saw the house advertised, I think the house was advertised for £1600 and by the time I, they saw who it was purchasing, it had gone to £2000 and odd, so anyhow I still went through with purchase because I wanted it."

The situation had changed by the Seventies, which brought more of the Windrush Generation migrants to Northamptonshire. As London filled up people were offered relocation packages to help them settle in Northamptonshire. Many people who were professionals, such as teachers, or who had a trade, such as welders, were offered relocation packages. The new arrivals were attracted by the clean, open spaces and the affordability of the property compared with London. Juliana Hall, whose parents came from Barbados and who grew up in London, explains why she came to live in Wellingborough in 1978: "I saw an advert in the paper about houses in Wellingborough for, like, six thousand and you think, 'Well I'll get a house for that amount'... we went to see the agents who were promoting the houses in Wellingborough. He said that if we come up to Wellingborough we won't find that they are prejudiced against our colour."

As individuals started to settle they began to develop social networks and look for ways to be entertained.

Ulric Gravesande talked about going to clubs in the Fifties: "When I came to Northampton there were two or three places in Northampton doing big band and I would just like to go, pay my money, go in and sit down and listen, and sit with the chaps and have a chat. But sometimes they wouldn't allow us to go, you know. Some time they'd say 'Oh well, tonight is not your night you can't come in, stay outside, stay out and listen to the music and then go home'." Informal networks developed with people meeting together to play sports on the Racecourse, or at each other's homes to chat on a Sunday afternoon, or for dances in basements or rented halls on a Saturday night.

Joe Dixon, who has lived in Northampton since 1958, described the first Caribbean club in Northampton: "What they used to do, they used to have coach outings in the holidays...and domino tournaments, and that's how the United Social Club was first started." It provided something of a lifeline for the members and became an integral part of the life in the town, not just for Black people but also for White. Carl McFarlane remembered a later period, after the move to Green Street: "...in the winter, we all used to go down the Club, and they have a lot of dominos down there... Some people would be play, would be throwing darts, some people would be playing skittles while others might be upstairs dancing because we always have music there and some people go up to dance. So there's always something to occupy your time."

The United Social Club cricket team played a big part in the life of the club and was incredibly successful. Marlene Codner talked about the cricket team: "I've been supporting them now for the last 30 years...if you go back to 1977, they've won Northampton Town League now for about eighteen, nineteen years. Yeah they've won it for so many years. They win the Garnet Cup, the Town League Cup." Sport was an important part of the life of the Caribbean migrants. Northampton also had the very successful amateur football team, the Persuaders, which was made up mainly of players originating from the Caribbean. A more

United Social Club cricket team

detailed account of the Black presence in Northamptonshire sport, and of the many other Caribbean community groups which developed after the United Social Club, can be read in Chapters Eleven and Thirteen of this book.

Church was a vital strand in the social life of most Caribbean people. Debbie Brown's parents came from Nevis but grew up in Bedford, and she talked about the large role religion played in her life as she grew up: "Well, my Mum was into the church, she used to go to church, so a lot of our social life was around the church. Sunday, twice a day; Tuesday, prayer meeting; Thursday, prayer meeting; Friday, young people's meeting - so you know, the church filled up a lot of your time." Religion plays an important part of Caribbean culture and was central to social activities and education. Arrivals looked for congregations to join, but many found they were disregarded. George Cleghorn talked about his experience looking for a church in Northampton: "I wandered around a little. I been to one or two churches before, just on occasion, and see the response that they give to you. And some of them didn't even want to see you come into their church because the seat that you go and sit in, you know, it's a family seat that belong to a family... but I as a stranger goes to a church, see the church, and I want to go to church... When they came and want to sit there, they couldn't get to sit... It came out that they didn't want Black people to come because they take away the church."

Some Caribbean settlers had more positive experiences of Northampton churches. Morcea Walker's family found a spiritual home at the Abington United Reform Church. Cynthia Dyer and others joined the Anglican Christchurch, in the Wellingborough Road area of Northampton where many Black families lived. Ivan and Mavis Bryan eventually entered the Sacred Heart Catholic Church at Weston Favell, converting to Catholicism as they felt accepted there. Others held prayer meetings in each other's houses until they were ready to establish their own churches in Northampton and Wellingborough. These were often Pentecostal Free Churches which resembled the churches in the Caribbean.

The New Testament Church of God was the first of several new churches which were founded in the 1960s to serve predominantly Black congregations. Elka Sterling recalls the arrival of two evangelist missionaries from the Rugby New Testament Church of God to begin the church in Vernon Terrace School Hall in September 1962. Soon Sunday morning services and a Sunday school were well established, with Pastor Grant as the first Minister. Encouragement and support were offered by a lay-preacher and Sunday school teacher, Mr Woolly of Monks Park Church, who was "different from other White Reverends in that he was a real Christian, humanitarian and receptive toward Black people". Local deacons soon included Richard Heath (just quoted) and George Cleghorn. After several changes of premises the New Testament

New Testament Church of God, Overstone 1987

Church of God moved into the impressive buildings of the former College Street Baptist Chapel, where the congregation had been active supporters of the anti-slavery movement a hundred years earlier. The Church of God Assembly began in Northampton in approximately 1964, under the leadership of Bishop Henrickets from Nottingham. From Stimpson Avenue School Hall they moved on to Clare Street, where they still worship. The Church of God of Prophecy was set up in Northampton in the mid-1970s, as part of a larger organisation established in London and Birmingham in the 1960s. It has been worshipping in Perry Street for the past twenty-six years, as one of a group of Caribbean-led churches which continue to serve their local communities to the present day.

Settlers in Northampton needed spiritual support, but they had more down-to-earth needs as well. One further challenge to the lifestyle of the Windrush migrants was the food, again an important part Caribbean culture and identity. May Green talks about her disappointment with British food in 1959, and how it has changed over the years: "When we came over here, food was abolished where we're concerned. I was out of food because all you could get was rice, that's the nearest thing that we would get to our food, was rice and sweet potato, I mean English potato we call it Irish potato back home. And that was the only thing because it's...afterwards that our food started to come to this country. And then, from starting from the West Indies to come, food coming from all over the world now."

In the beginning, getting hold of the right ingredients was very difficult. Cynthia Dyer remembers a man coming round on a bicycle to sell food. However eventually other retailers started to cash in. Marjorie Bradshaw remembers: "When they started selling the Caribbean food, they didn't even know how to sell it. They used to sell it cheap...and then after a while, you will go to them and you will tell them, 'You must buy okra, you must buy sweet potato, you must buy yam and corn meal.' And you tell them, you know what I mean, and saltfish and ackee and all them sort of things. So you know they keep buying the things then until they are sold, they doing good out of us." Many families kept their culinary traditions of eating rice and peas, soup and other Caribbean dishes, but also ate English dishes.

The struggle to adapt and survive challenged the Windrush Generation's received definition of Britishness. Realising that they were not completely accepted as British citizens, and yet being something else, people had to negotiate the subtleties of their multiple identities. Norma McFarlane highlighted this sense of ambivalence: "I think I am a mixture of everything. I know I'm a very strong Black woman because I had to be, you know...I see myself as a Jamaican but I see myself as British because I've live most of my life here, so I feel that I should feel British but I don't feel that I'll be accepted."

In the Seventies and Eighties the younger generation gradually became more radicalised, and were searching for a positive identity. Trevor Hall (now called Ras Jabulani) talked about the search for self-definition. He related his parents' struggles to make a life in Britain, their sense of disappointment and disillusionment, and his own fight to gain acceptance. This led many to search further back to their African roots to find self-definition. Ashley Sinclair talked about early Black consciousness movements in London, and their lessons in Black History: "I got an invitation to actually come to a meeting, as I was told. This meeting was going on a Sunday afternoon, talking some wonderful things about Black History...first of all I was in disbelief. I just couldn't believe the Egyptians were Black and that Black people had done so many wonderful things...I came to this awareness that there's been a real deception in my, how many years did I spend in school, seven years in school. I was taught history and I was taught nothing that validated Black people. I myself had actually gone through the process of being completely devalued and having to somehow find some credibility within myself and actually had gone through a really awkward way of actually preserving my self esteem which is a denial, you know, of my identity."

In Northamptonshire this rise in Black consciousness materialised as the Matta Fancanta Movement. Primarily a youth movement, it gave Black people a place to go and find a voice. Ras Jabulani explains how MFM grew from a few people meeting informally into a fully-fledged centre with its own programme: "As youths we had our own ideas, we wanted...our own kind of freedom to express ourselves, but we didn't have the access to venues...we decided we would, you know, let's sit down, let's get something more tangible together and start teaching ourselves more about ourselves, about our history and so forth. Because we had, we have a history which we are to be proud of, as Black people, you see, because our story goes from ancient days." After some difficulty getting premises, MFM started to squat in the old Salvation Army Citadel building in the centre of Northampton. The movement had its roots in Rastafarianism and was expressed in music: "We had a place we could play our music...we had a place where we can teach, we had Black History classes going on and so forth. Eventually we managed to get certain skilled people who was within us training the youngsters in various other things."

The Matta Fancanta Movement made a break with the older generation's loyalty to Britishness by reclaiming their African roots. This involved exploring music, fashion, hairstyles, religion in the

Members of MFM

form of Rastafarianism, and Black History. Such radical explorations often created tensions with the older generation. Matta Fancanta – meaning "Come Guard Yourself Against Self-Destruction" – began in 1977 as a place where young Black people could explore their identity. Financial support was eventually obtained from the Borough Council for MFM's youth work and measures against youth unemployment. After many years delivering a wide-ranging programme of training and support for young people in Northampton, the organisation disbanded following management difficulties.

MFM and other Black consciousness movements in Britain tried to educate young Black people partly because they believed that British schools were failing to meet their needs. Evidence from the Northamptonshire oral history archive bears out this belief. Almost all the Caribbean settlers who arrived here as school children suffered an education disrupted by racist bullying and low teacher expectations. The experiences of the second generation were often equally negative.

For a start, British teachers had no knowledge of the differences between education in the Caribbean and in Britain, and therefore failed to understand the needs of children moving from one system to another. Children in the Caribbean followed a British syllabus and learnt a lot about Britain, but they were used to a much stricter learning environment. In Jamaica, punishment for any bad behaviour began at school and continued at home. As Joe Dixon put it: "Teacher told you what you were doing and you had to do it. Coz they had the backing from your parents if you did anything wrong, you get a good hiding and if you went home and said anything, you would get another one, coz you must have done something wrong why you got that hiding."

Children learnt their lessons well, both in school and in church, and were astonished by the low expectations of behaviour and academic achievement which they found in many British schools. At the same time, their education suffered from the negative judgements which teachers applied to the Black children in their classes, whether they had been born in Britain or the Caribbean. Norma McFarlane remembers her arrival at a London school in 1962: "You'd sit at the back most of the time. Even if there was a seat at the front it would be re-arranged that you sit at the back. And the only thing they were interested in, if you could run, or you could jump. If you could do any of that you were well in." The teachers were unapproachable and "you weren't picked out to answer questions. Like, you put your hand up and then, you know... I found that weird." Another problem was the streaming of classes by ability: "You were just put in a lower class...I think maybe that's how they looked at it then, to say 'Well, you're not speaking perfect English so you've not got the ability', when often it was not that way." Monica Noel had similar experiences in Yorkshire in the 1960s: "I had one teacher who said to me I'd never pass an O-level...she refused to put me in for O-level, saying 'because of your grammar you'll never pass an O-level'. Yet I end up having four O-levels and a degree."

Bullying was even harder to endure, and was experienced by almost all the Caribbean children who entered British schools in the 1960s and 1970s. Ray Campbell, who came to Northampton as an eleven-year-old in 1966, recalls: "at the school, you know, my reality was fighting to survive and that's how I would describe being at school from start to finish...it was just as if they viewed it as the norm to either pick on you or beat you up or whatever, and my brother he had a similar experience." For Ron Frater, arriving in London in the same year, "it was horrible, horrible starting at school and I think there were only two Black boys in the whole school". At secondary school a few months later, Ron was advised by his father to stand up for himself, and earned a measure of respect by winning a fight with a fourteen-year-old bully: "I leathered him in the end...I don't think it was just him, it was just the behaviour of people towards me since I came to England, just the frustration just came out and it was a release for me really." Girls were sometimes involved in playground fights as well, but usually found themselves victimised through name-calling and other, less obvious kinds of bullying. Over the years, many children found their own survival strategies and sometimes even made friends with former tormentors.

Very few members of the Windrush Generation share Morcea Walker's entirely positive memories of school and schooling. After joining her father in Britain in 1958, she quickly excelled in all areas of learning. At secondary school there were few Black pupils, and the head teacher held firm views: "Any element of racism, it was made quite clear you come and you complain." Morcea went on to become Head Girl, and to pass all the examinations needed for entry to teacher training college. She arrived in Northampton as one of the town's first Black teachers in 1973, and was soon making an impact as a positive role model for Black children. The responsibilities of a pioneering Black teacher extended beyond the classroom, and before long Morcea found herself giving informal advice and encouragement to many Caribbean families. In 1974 she combined with Ivan Bryan and others to launch the West Indian supplementary school, the West Indian Parents Association, and its very successful summer playscheme. In 1987 Morcea Walker was promoted from the classroom to the Northamptonshire County Council's advisory service. As Equalities Advisor and Supplementary Schools Co-ordinator, she is nowadays responsible for twenty-three supplementary schools throughout Northamptonshire, serving children and parents from many parts of the world.

Morcea Walker story-telling

The Windrush Generation had very mixed experiences of education, and the same is true of their encounters with the Police. In Northamptonshire, as elsewhere, there were plenty of incidents which soured relationships and confirmed the existence of the "institutional racism" highlighted by the murder of London teenager Stephen Lawrence in 1997. A number of strong individuals from the local Caribbean community decided from the 1970s onwards that the best way to ensure fairer treatment for the public was to change the Police Force from within. June White Gulley was Northamptonshire's first Black African Caribbean police officer in 1978. When she went for interview at the Police Headquarters at Wootton Hall, she made it clear from the start that she did not intend to sacrifice her Black identity: "As my training sergeant, even years later when I left the Force, he says, 'June, I never forget yer...you came to the interview with a headscarf on your head and a pair of sandals on...and you sat there reading *Roots*'. That's the book I went and bought." June's promising police career ended when her own brother was ill-treated by a local police officer; however her son is now a successful member of the Metropolitan Police.

June Gulley and her son

Ron Frater also decided to join the Police, in 1984. This was not an easy decision, since he knew that he would meet with criticisms from within the Black community as well as "antagonism from the White community". He himself had been frequently stopped and searched under the infamous 'sus' laws, but nothing had prepared him for the prejudices which he encountered within the Police Force itself. After a difficult start in London, Ron moved to Northampton where he was soon joined by Ray Campbell: "He started telling me the horror stories of some of his experiences in London. I said, 'Well, I tell you what, it's out of the frying pan into the fire because it's not much different here.' As our numbers slowly increased solidarity sort of built up between us." Together, Ron Frater and Ray Campbell have

Ron Frater at work

played a pivotal role in developing the Black Police Association. The Northamptonshire branch was the first to be established outside London. Its founders have also triumphed over the odds to achieve career distinction. Ron Frater was awarded an MBE 'For Services to the Police' in 2001, and was 'Northamptonshire Police Officer of the Year' in 2002. Ray Campbell was Northamptonshire's first Black Sergeant in 1987, and retired in 2006 as Superintendent and holder of the Queen's Police Medal for distinguished service.

Despite some disappointment and disillusionments, the majority of the Windrush Generation succeeded in creating homes and careers for themselves in Britain. In Northamptonshire there are retired teachers, social workers, health workers, transport workers, church workers, tradesmen, retailers, business leaders and town councillors who have all been part of that wave of migration. Their children and grandchildren are to be found in every kind of local employment, and at the heart of many community organisations. These achievements can be attributed to the first generation's sense of pride, determination and stoicism. However, there has been some sense of loss as their experiences in Britain have led them to redefine their own identities; this is also true for the second and third generations. Juliana Hall talked about having to qualify her status as a British person because of being Black: "I suppose, like my generation... what you sort of had shoved at you a lot of the time, you know, coz... you know, 'Where are you from?'. 'I was born here.' 'Where are your parents from?' So automatically you have to...get that connection with the West Indies, you know, so I think that's just what they've come up with. So I just say, 'Well, I'm Black British, my parents are from Barbados.'"

June White Gulley, like many other Black people born in Britain, reaches into history for her definition: "I describe myself as a Black British born of Jamaican parents from African Ancestors." On the other hand the overtly racist behaviour of the Fifties and Sixties has been reconfigured. Morcea Walker talked about the changes in racism: "Sometimes I sort of think the Fifties and Sixties, although they may appear harder on paper, were easier to deal with you know. I think I said before, you know, if somebody said to you, 'Nigger, leave my country'...it was horrible, but it was like, in-your-face and you'd know where it was. I think we're into the subtle racism bit now as time progresses."

Although racism still exists, there is a feeling that the presence of Black people has become accepted. Ulric Gravesande said: "In view of the fact that there are so many Black people now in this town...I believe that the people of the town have learnt to accept the fact that we've got to live a life together and they are more accommodating than they have been, many years ago." Janet Douglas-Hall remarked:

"We have to live together, you know. Because you have four generations, in this Northampton I know the four generations in Black families and they ain't going nowhere."

Sylvia Bowmer's marriage gave her an understanding of the wide-ranging nature of human prejudice. She learnt many years ago to silence any comments on her choice of husband with the remark: "I didn't (get) married to a White man, I'm married to a man. Full stop." Nowadays, "the younger generation, it seems as if they are having a breakthrough, because the amount of children that is being born between Black and White now, there is no stopping".

Marlene Codner took an optimistic view of race relations in Britain: "Now we are very, very much a multicultural society. Things are not just looked at in terms of Whites, it's just looked at in the broad picture." Juliana Hall made a similar point. Black people have had a positive influence on British culture, from food to music: "I think it has become a lot more multicultural and multiculturalism, I think, is an accepted part or a more accepted part of British culture." On the other hand, she noted that there are still places in Britain which do not have any Black people at all and there are still people who need to be educated about race issues: "I think Black people have influenced certain parts of the country, but there are a lot of parts that have not been influenced at all I would think".

Debbie Brown noted that Black culture is sometimes being adopted by White people and becoming part of the mainstream: "There seems to be a new wave of consciousness coming... there's a new culture of the hip-hop style and everyone is going for it and some of them, I think, feel that it's been taken away from them; because we started it first sort of thing... this is our thing. But you know, the young White kids are doing it as well, and then I think it, well...isn't it a good thing though, you know, that we all sort of fusing together and it's all coming into one."

Since the Windrush migrants made their journey to Britain there have been significant challenges and changes, not just for the migrants themselves but for their descendants and for Britain as a nation. This journey has not been simply from discrimination to acceptance, but has involved dealing with ambivalence, and negotiating and redefining identities and ideas about nationhood and culture. The Windrush Generation, their children and grandchildren have had an enduring impact upon the cultural landscape of Britain.

Northampton Carnival

Further Reading:

ACES, *Cold Arrival* (Northampton: ACES, 1998)

P. Fryer, *Staying Power. The History of Black People in Britain* (London: Pluto Press, 1984)

P. Gilroy, *Black Britain: A Photographic History* (London: Saqi, 2007)

D. Hinds, *Journey to an Illusion: The West Indian in Britain* (London: Heinemann, 1966)

M. Phillips and T. Phillips, *Windrush: the irresistible rise of multi-racial Britain* (London: Harper Collins, 1998)

R. Ramdin, *Re-Imaging Britain: 500 Years of Black and Asian History* (London: Pluto Press, 1999)

B. Richardson (ed.), *Tell It Like It Is: How Our Schools Fail Black Children* (London: Bookmarks Publications, 2005)

Websites

The Northamptonshire Black History Association's database gives references to the individuals mentioned in this chapter, with some biographical information. Many other members of the Windrush Generation, and the community organisations they founded, are also listed by name: www.northants-black-history.org.uk

Moving Here (Migration Histories) provides information, stories and a picture gallery related to the Caribbean community in Britain: www.movinghere.org.uk

Primary sources

The interviews quoted in the chapter are in the Northamptonshire Black History Project's oral history archive at the Northamptonshire Record Office. These interviews have been fully transcribed and summarised, and are available for listening and reading by the general public.

Only a few interviews are directly referred to in the chapter, from the much larger number which together provide its main evidence.

This chapter was written by Anne-Marie Sandos

Northamptonshire's South Asian Communities

British Asians are the largest ethnic minority in Northamptonshire. This umbrella term is used to describe British citizens who originated from or are descendants of migrants from the Southern Asian states of India, Pakistan, Bangladesh or Sri Lanka. The 2001 Census recorded a Northamptonshire population of 629,676, of whom 2 per cent were British Asians, compared to an overall 4 per cent of the total British population. The highest numbers locally were concentrated in the urban centres: 4.5 per cent of the Wellingborough population were of South Asian origin, compared to 0.4 per cent in rural East Northamptonshire.

The majority of Northamptonshire's South Asian population settled here in the 1960s and early 1970s and were from the Punjab region of Northern India and Pakistan, and Gujerat on the north-west coast of India. In 1967 and 1972 the governments of Kenya and Uganda decided to drive out their Asian populations in order to create better economic opportunities for Black Africans. These official "Africanisation" policies resulted in the forced migration to Britain of large numbers of East African Asians who were British passport-holders. Northampton also has a significant Bangladeshi community which began to grow after the 1971 civil war in what was then East Pakistan. Continuing political disruption and poverty led to increased migration which peaked in the 1980s, as family members joined the pioneers.

Alad Miah, Bangladeshi chef

This chapter draws upon interviews carried out by the Northamptonshire Black History Project with members of the post-1960 generation of Asian settlers. It attempts to reflect the diverse origins and backgrounds of the interviewees, as they describe in their own words their experience of life in Northamptonshire and how their varied cultures and beliefs have adapted and evolved. One common feature is an involvement in grassroots community organisations that were set up initially to support new arrivals. A more detailed account of some of these organisations can be found in Chapter Thirteen.

The settlers who constitute Northamptonshire's present day South Asian population were not the first to come here. Settlers from the Indian subcontinent have been coming to live and work in Northamptonshire since the founding of the East India Company in 1600 (see Chapter Two). It might also be possible to describe the Romany people (gypsies) as the earliest known settlers from the Indian subcontinent. The Roma and Sinti are believed to have originated in parts of what is now North India and Pakistan. They started moving westward around 1000 AD, mixing with central Asians and Europeans on the way, and reaching the British Isles during the late Middle Ages. After 1600, wealthy English families returning home from India often brought back their domestic servants or ayahs. Numbers increased after the establishment of the British Raj and Crown Rule from 1858. Small communities of Indian seamen, or lascars as they were known, began to grow in the major British ports, particularly in the East End of London. After having been recruited to replace vacancies on East India Company ships, many were refused passage home and marooned in London. With the advent of steam-powered shipping in the 1870s, the lascars soon monopolised the boiler-stoking work considered too heavy and dirty by European sailors. Poorly paid Indian seafarers became indispensable to the British maritime labour force and crucially helped keep supply lines open during the First and Second World Wars (see Chapter Seven).

Migration increased following the break-up of the British Empire after 1945. The introduction of the British Nationality Act in 1948 gave all Commonwealth subjects British citizenship and the right of free entry. It has been estimated that by 1949 there were no more than eight thousand settlers from the Indian sub-continent in Britain, of whom one thousand were doctors. By 1955 numbers had already increased to roughly fifty-five thousand Indians and Pakistanis. The post-war industrial boom, together with the relaxation of stringent controls on the issuing of passports by the Indian government, drew migrants in larger numbers. Workers were needed to rebuild Britain's bombed-out towns and devastated economy. The British government encouraged the migration of semi-skilled and unskilled young men from rural areas, particularly from Pakistan. Typically, they were unfamiliar with the language and culture of Britain and they found work in the textiles or steel industries. Following a similar pattern to the new migrants from the Caribbean, single men were often the first to arrive. They intended to make their fortunes and return home, but then settled permanently in Britain with wives and families following them here. Medical staff were recruited for the newly formed National Health Service, as the British had established medical schools in the sub-continent which conformed to British standards of medical care.

Race riots in 1958 led to calls for the limitation of migration and in 1962 the Commonwealth Immigrants Act limited the numbers of unskilled workers. Commonwealth citizens now had to either be in possession of a valid work voucher issued by the Ministry of Labour, or be able to prove they were a bona fide student, or enter as a short-term visitor who could support themselves, or be a dependent accompanying an entrant or joining somebody already resident in Britain. Fearful of even stricter controls, many Asian people already here sent for their families. The new restrictions meant that the adult male newcomers were increasingly skilled professionals, eager to find work and establish a home in Britain.

Arriving in Northamptonshire

Most of the original migrants of the 1960s and 1970s came indirectly to Northamptonshire, often via London and Leicester where family members were already settled. Reasons for coming varied, but most hoped for better opportunities and an improvement in their economic prospects. Northamptonshire had many thriving local industries at this time. After Northampton was designated a "new town" in 1968 there was major housing expansion to the east of the town, mainly to help accommodate London's overflow population. Over the period of the Northampton Development Corporation twenty thousand new homes were built, and more than forty thousand new residents arrived, including the South Asians.

It is now time to turn away from the general picture of Asian settlement in order to listen to the memories of some individuals. The stories which follow illustrate the diversity of Asian experience, as well as bringing the statistics to life. People came to Northamptonshire for varied reasons, and their early experiences reflected their different origins and circumstances.

Niranjan Jani came to Wellingborough in the early 1980s after arriving in Britain several years earlier. He was born in Surat, Gujarat, in 1949. His brother-in-law came here to study in 1955 and settled in Leicester where Naranjan's sister joined him in 1969. Niranjan had gained a degree in Commerce and worked in India as a banker: "When I graduated in 1972 I started writing to my sister and showing my ambition that I wish to come to UK and study and have a better life." His brother-in-law helped secure Niranjan's admission to Leicester Polytechnic and submitted a Sponsorship Declaration: "With those documents I went to the British High Commission in Bombay." A thorough medical check-up and x-rays followed: "There was a fear of TB I think. I thought, God knows what will come out and probably that will stop me getting into Britain. Everything went well."

Chaman Kalyan was born in 1944 in Mandhali, in the Punjab: "It is a medium-sized village, where there were not so many facilities and people were just living on agriculture." His father was in the border security force and the only time he could spend at home was his six weeks of holiday: "We were lucky because we had only two children in my family so we were relatively quite well off...There was not much education. Given a cluster of four or five villages there was only one primary school... children had to walk three or four mile away on feet." Charman developed an early interest in politics and was selected aged 22 as a candidate for the Punjab Assembly. Though tipped "to win that seat ... a rich man came and they gave the seat to him". In 1967 he achieved a degree in Economics, Political Science and English, only to be told, on applying to join the elite Indian Civil Service, that "because of my political participation. I have been disqualified. If I am not able to become something here then I will not live in this country!" In 1971 he was persuaded to move to England. Friends helped him to find accommodation: "They supported me because I could not find a job for nearly three months." Living in Swindon, he eventually found work on a building site: "It was quite hard work but there were Irish workers with me." The Irishmen complained he was "doing too much work" and so "they taught me some tactics, how to spend your time while showing that you are doing your job".

Chaman Kalyan, Council Leader

Yousuf Miah arrived in Northampton as a ten-year-old in 1986, together with his parents and five brothers and sisters. They came from Syhlet, Bangladesh: "Just before we came there was a lot of unrest. The decision to move here was more to do with personal safety rather than a better lifestyle."

First Impressions

Many South Asians recall the dramatic change in climate as their first impression on arrival in Britain. Niranjan Jani arrived in late summer: "Very cold! I had about three and a half weeks to settle in a completely new country, adapt to the new environment and so on.... I went to the Polytechnic with lots of woollen clothes... this was the first week in September." Shashi Dholakia, arriving from Africa, recalls: "I came in late February when it was bitterly cold. Wintertime, you know, and having stayed in a warm climate - Kenya and India - and coming to awesome cold mornings of England, I didn't particularly like it. I felt quite alienated."

Nitha Padeep, a nurse from Kerala in the south of India, travelled to Northampton in 2003: "I came here in the wintertime and it was very cold compared to tropical Kerala, but what troubled me most was the bright light of the sun so low in the winter sky. I needed to wear a cap and sun glasses." However the climate change was not quite so drastic for everybody. Farhat Lateef grew up in the Pakistani cities of Karachi and then Lahore, and had experienced severe winters there. She arrived to a chilly British autumn after recently spending some time in the snow-covered mountains of Kashmir.

Sarwat Khakhar

Sarwat Khakhar's first encounter with the British public was not a pleasant experience. She was born in Nairobi of a prosperous Hindu family, her great-grandfather having come from India in the 1880s to help build the Kenyan railway system. After attending secretarial college Sarwat went on to a good job working for the United Nations. When she applied with her Muslim husband to migrate to Canada, there was a job offer for Sarwat at the UN Office in Montreal, but his application was rejected. Eventually they both moved to England instead. Sarwat travelled alone in 1970, ahead of her husband: "It was a shock to the system, the moment you enter this country. First of all at the airport. I was on my own. Nobody would support me, nobody would give me any help. I had a baby two months old in my hand, and a daughter three years old. And I was literally struggling with my suitcases. If I asked anybody [for help] people just turn their faces away. It was quite degrading. That look they give you to say 'What the hell are you doing here?' That was the attitude. But my father was here because he'd brought my younger brothers for education. As soon as I saw his face at the airport my feelings changed. He was my own Dad, and I just couldn't care what people say or look at me. He had a small room for us, bed-sit type of thing, just one room. I had to share kitchen and bath room with other families, which was again a shock to my system."

Dipana Patel's family came here in 1972 as refugees from Uganda: "I was about five years old when my family left Uganda, following the Idi Amin regime, and we had some other family in Wellingborough and we arrived at a camp somewhere in Wales. I don't remember the exact location. And I remember living there for about three weeks in a holiday camp and then arriving here as a five-year-old in Wellingborough." The family had been comfortably off in Uganda but now her parents had to start all over again. In 1977 her father bought a business in Irthlingborough: "I moved from having grown up in what I thought was cosmopolitan Wellingborough to sleepy Irthlingborough where we were the only Asian family."

Working Lives and Home-Making

The priorities of most male settlers were to secure employment and find a home, then it would be possible to consider family life and bringing over wives and children. For many newly arrived wives, sometimes with young families, it was a difficult and lonely life without the security and support of an extended family. Some single men enjoyed their initial freedom from family and cultural restraints, but problems finding work were common.

Professional and educational qualifications were often not recognised and retraining was necessary. Many people were forced to take work for which they were over-qualified. Some faced discrimination before finding suitable housing, but for those coming to Northamptonshire this was less of a problem than elsewhere as the house-building programme kept pace with the growing population in the early 1970s. However, wider economic downturns during the 1970s and 1980s coincided with an upsurge in racist politics and hostility towards newcomers, especially those who spoke a different language and had such varied and distinctive customs and appearances.

Niranjan Jani completed the two-year Higher Education Diploma in Business Studies in Leicester and applied for four jobs with local companies, taking up a position as a graduate trainee with a car component distributor. Financial independence was very welcome but his student visa was running out and he was obliged to apply for permanent residence. Niranjan's brother-in-law was once again able to help out, arranging an appointment with their local MP. With his support, and a letter of appointment and references from his employer, Niranjan's application was successful: "I had a passport with a stamp to stay permanently in the UK. And that was the happiest moment of my life I think." He returned to India in October 1977 to marry, and his wife Shobna joined him in Leicester in November 1979. Shobna found work as a library assistant and they were soon able to buy a home of their own. After several years in the drawing office of an engineering factory, Niranjan went on to work for a Building Society in a predominantly Asian area of the city.

After being made redundant on the building site, then doing a stint with a firm manufacturing agricultural machines, Chaman Kalyan found a "nice and clean and light job" working on a conveyor belt, packing cosmetics for Woolworth's: "After a few weeks I was made deputy foreman." He moved to Leicester,

Jamila Amar

where his cousin and her family had settled, before coming to Northampton: "I had friends here... There were three families here and I stayed with them. We were like a family of brothers and sisters." They all enjoyed listening to Indian music and socialising, and would sometimes visit the seaside: "hire the bus and all the families go together". Eventually he got a job on the buses, "because they were very, very short of conductors and bus drivers".

Jamila Amar and her husband came to Britain as refugees from Uganda. After three years with relatives in Blackburn they moved to Southall in London, but had problems finding a house. Unwilling to take up the offer of a council house in faraway Putney, they were given the option of moving to a "new town" - either Peterborough, Northampton, or Milton Keynes: "My husband already had a sister in Northampton, and my husband said 'okay, let's go and visit my sister and see what we're going to do'. So we came to visit and my sister-in-law said 'there's so many jobs going here and you can get a job

in about five, six weeks time, so why do you want to stay there?' And really he didn't like London, my husband is a very quiet type of person, he doesn't like noisy places. When I came from Southall I said 'such a neat and clean place'. We both went to work for British Timken's, we worked there for three years and then we moved on."

Saeed Ahmed Pirzada, a law graduate, responded to a government advertisement in India calling for qualified people to work in Britain. He applied for a work voucher and came here in 1963: "When I came I couldn't first find job you know. My qualifications were not recognised at all, although they asked

for a law graduate. I came and my qualifications were negated, they were not acknowledged. I had to...start work in a factory, a couple of years I did odd jobs.' He remembers that his fellow-workers asked the question "why did he come?", to which he replied "I didn't come, I was invited". Eventually he found a job as a customs officer at Heathrow Airport.

Meharban Plahay trained as a teacher in Nairobi, Kenya. A Commonwealth bursary allowed him to travel to England and continue his studies for a year in Sheffield. A teaching post was offered in Bedford, but he encountered problems when

Meharban and Mohinder Plahay

trying to find accommodation: "We went to the first house and the lady looked at me, she had never seen an Indian before, especially a turbaned Sikh, and straight away she said 'sorry I haven't got a place'. So, moving along to the next one, there was a lady sort of sweeping up the yard, the forecourt of her house and we asked her where so-and-so was. And she said 'yes that's me', so I said 'well I am the gentleman who is looking for a house'. She just walked in the house and slammed the door and didn't say a word." Housing options improved greatly when he applied for a teaching job in Corby. The local housing department promptly offered a choice of four new houses, and he was soon able to organise travel arrangements for his wife and two young children still in India.

Another trained teacher, Farhat Lateef, had to abandon hopes of a teaching career in Britain: "I was a graduate from Pakistan... but they said the graduation from there is not recognised here." In 1971 her family arranged her marriage to a cousin who had studied in England and was working as a civil servant at the Old Bailey. They lived in Streatham and she worked as a salesperson for Avon until the birth of her son. In 1974 the family moved to the Abington area in Northampton. Mr Lateef commuted to London for five years before taking a job at the Crown Court in Northampton. He also worked as a translator for social services and the police throughout Northamptonshire. With her husband now home earlier and able to help with childcare, Farhat took an evening job at the new Tesco's at Weston Favell. She also started helping out as a volunteer, and from 1985 worked as a waged bi-lingual teaching assistant at Vernon Terrace school where her own children studied.

Sarwat Khakhar experienced great loneliness in her early days in Britain: "Yes, it was very different here. I was brought up in an extended family. My Granddad had a huge house and he obviously expected all his sons and their families to live in that house, so it catered for about three or four families. So all the cousins were like sisters, played together. We didn't need to go out because we had a lot of company around." She had second thoughts about settling here: "It was such a lonely life to start with. It was very, very lonely. I used to ring my Dad to say 'Why have I moved?'. When I came there were very few Asian families in Northampton. For many years my children, my daughter and my son were the only ones in the class. A few times they would come home and say - so and so would say 'Paki' or 'go back home'. My son had a lot of problems as a teenager. Some of the skinheads would come and try to attack him. Who would come to help him? Afro-Caribbean lads."

Dipana Patel also struggled, as the only Asian student at her Irthlingborough school: "Because my father had a sweetie shop, all the children were friends with me and I thought I could bribe them with sweets. And I was fine for the first two months, and then in my second year I was subject to some horrific bullying. Horrific racist bullying. And my father, being the man he was, wouldn't believe it and said that I had to sort it out myself. I would be called names, my books would be ripped apart and nobody would want to partner me." Things improved when a teacher moved her to a different class and she learnt to stand up for herself: "I just remember picking up their book and saying 'I will rip your text book up. You're ripping my note book, I'll just rip up the textbook, then you will answer to that.'"

Dipana Patel

Meharban Plahay's son was the only Sikh at his school in Corby, but his experience was far more positive. Mrs Plahay remembers: "He had a wonderful time there. Sometimes he would come home without his turban, sort of wrapped around his head or neck. And then his teacher one day sent a note home to ask me to see her. He was a very boisterous lad. She said 'I wish I could put it back on. Could you teach me how to do it?' I showed her how to put the turban on, and from then on whenever the turban came off she put it on."

More recent Asian settlers are still coping with some of the same issues of work, housing and education. However the rise of a powerful Indian economy has opened up new options. Nitha Pradeep travelled to Northampton in 2003 from Kottayam in Kerala, southern India. She is a trained nurse and was recruited by Northampton General Hospital through an employment agency, together with forty others, mostly from Christian backgrounds. Representatives of Northampton General Hospital interviewed her in Kottayam and she was offered a contract for two years and a four-year work permit visa. Nitha hoped there would be greater opportunities for career development in Northampton. Following a short adaptation course, she started work on the medical wards. At the end of her first year she returned home for three months to marry Mahood, who returned with her to Northampton. Like many earlier migrants, Mahood found that his Occupational Therapy qualifications were not recognised here and he has been obliged to take low-waged, unskilled warehouse work. Their three-year-old son Satia will be returning home with Pradeep's mother, who is here helping with childcare. Nitha and her husband feel that the schooling here is too relaxed, whereas "In India he will learn to speak our local language (Malayalam), Hindi and English." Nursing in Northampton is not as rewarding as it was when she first started: "My grades and pay have improved but morale is low, there is too much politics and there is a lot of stress. We want to go back in a few years. It is too expensive here, the cost of living and particularly housing. Mahood will be able to get a good job very easily, and I will look after our home."

Social, Cultural and Religious Life

The South Asian settlers of the 1960s and 1970s worked long hours and were busy raising young families. They had little free time or spare money available for leisure activities. The prohibitive expense of phone calls and flights home increased the desire for familiar sounds, smells and faces and any opportunities to create feelings of home were embraced through the celebration of weddings, recitals and festivals. Greater prosperity in more recent years has allowed for more outward signs of culture and community. Greater security and confidence has also enabled Asian settlers to participate more widely in British society.

After accepting a council house in Lings on the Eastern District of Northampton, Jamila Amar found her social life was restricted, but this changed as the South Asian population grew: "It was very quiet, the weekends and the holidays were very, very boring because we didn't have anywhere to go. We had to clean the house and this and that, but there was no social life for us... Eventually it started to grow, we saw lots of Asians coming in, we saw people having functions, we were having Muslim functions, we were having Hindu functions. I am a type of person who makes friends very easily and it started growing and now I don't want to leave Northampton!"

Many South Asians have participated actively in local politics, and Asian town councillors have served as Mayors both of Northampton and Wellingborough in recent years. Chaman Kalyan was able to resume his political activities after settling in Northampton. He was elected as a Labour Party councillor for Delapre and was on the Borough Council for many years: "Politics in this country is very tolerant. Once I was speaking on the Poll Tax and one Conservative shouted at me 'go back to India' and that was headline in the newspaper. This was the only incident in my twenty years in the Council...he apologised to me." When the National Front marched in Wellingborough in 1979, he demonstrated against them. He was later arrested and fined for adding to some 'NF' graffiti the words "...is an evil".

Sarwat Khakhar and her husband were instrumental in setting up the Asian Advisory Panel which helped new arrivals with access to housing, social security, advocacy and interpretation. With Farhat Lateef and others, she also helped establish Dostiyo (meaning "friendship") in Northampton. Based in offices near Debenham's in the Drapery, its aim was to promote "friendship and well being": it offered advice sessions on immigration, housing, and health, and provided creche facilities for families across the South Asian community.

Jamila Amar began working for Gharana Housing in Wellingborough as a meals-on-wheels supervisor in 1999, and went on to Nazarana which is a multicultural sheltered housing scheme for the frail and elderly. Niranjan Jani helped set up the Pravasi Mandal Asian Day Care Centre, which provides elderly day care services with the support of the Health Authority and Social Services.

Jinnah Day Centre, Northampton

Saeed Ahmed Pirzada has also been active in helping with the development of community organisations, including a mosque in Wellingborough and the Oriental Sports and Social Club. Yousuf Miah helped his father to organise support and social events for the Bangladeshi community in Northampton. The Islamic Pakistani Association was started by Farhat Lateef's husband and several of his friends in the 1980s. Based in Colwyn Road, Northampton, it included the Jinnah Day Centre which provided care for the elderly.

More can be read about all these voluntary organisations, and others, in Chapter Thirteen. Here, it is essential to acknowledge the importance of religion to Northamptonshire's Asian communities. Various national and local surveys have confirmed that South Asian settlers attach more significance to religion than any other section of society. For many settlers, religion has been a means of preserving their identity and helping to build a stronger community. For example, in the 2001 census 95 per cent of Wellingborough's South Asian population described themselves as Hindu, Muslim or Sikh, whereas only 81.7 per cent of Wellingborough's total population claimed any kind of religious faith. Religious community organisations are also described in Chapter Thirteen, including important groups founded by members of all the main South Asian religions.

Sikh festival of Vaisakhi, Northampton

Meanwhile recorded life histories convey the value of religious faith and practice for individuals, as well as for community groups and the voluntary social services they provide. Meharban Plahay, a Sikh, remembers how in the early days he used to celebrate religious events at home: "We used to travel to Northampton, so one festival in one's house and another in someone else's house." Sometimes he was obliged to travel as far afield as London in order to celebrate the Sikh festivals properly. With the support of the wider Sikh community, he eventually helped to open the Sikh temple in Kettering, which has been followed by temples in Wellingborough and Northampton.

Diwali in Northampton

Islam is a more diverse faith than it may appear to outsiders, with the principal Sunni and Shiah traditions including various further sub-divisions. The total number of Muslims living in Northampton has increased rapidly over the last ten years to more than ten thousand, as newcomers from Somalia, Nigeria, Turkey and Eastern Europe have joined the established Pakistani and Bangladeshi communities. There are now several active mosques in Northampton, and plans for more. Saeed Ahmed Pirzada compares life as a Muslim in Britain to his experience back home in Pakistan: "Here Muslims are from all over the world and when we congregate together it gives a sense of very multi-cultural feelings. To meet with different people is very exciting." The Wellingborough mosque has been particularly successful in drawing together Muslims from varied backgrounds.

Hinduism is the majority religion of India. Its many colourful gods and goddesses and diverse religious practices are becoming well-known across Britain, including within the main towns of Northamptonshire. Hindu culture and social life has many dimensions, including those linked to caste, sect, and regional tradition. Sham Naib, a Punjabi Hindu, came to Britain in 1967 to study at Nottingham University and train to be a teacher. He moved to Wellingborough in 1969 and recalls his first encounter with the existing Gujerati Hindu community: "I'd been here only a few years from home and still very much looked for my own people (laughed) so to speak. But I must say, right from the word go I knew they looked different from me and that's when I discovered they came from Gujerat. I discovered that they were very happy people already hiring halls, celebrating some of the Hindu festivals. That's when I went there and saw the happy jolly atmosphere and I thought well, this is a nice community and should be proud to be part of that."

Sham Naib involved himself with the Community Relations Council which was established in 1973, and the development of the Wellingborough communities' religious life. He recalls some anxieties associated with the opening of the Hindu temple: "although there were many that supported it, there were many Asians who thought that if we create our own separate identity through a temple then we, people would be alienated... and they wouldn't let us live here. There was a lot of fear." Northampton's Hindu Welfare Organisation, founded in 1996, is committed to enriching the lives of Northampton

Hindus, whilst at the same time "building an integrated and harmonious local society by building cohesion between Hindus and other communities".

Concerns over whether the promotion of a separate religious and cultural identity might hinder integration with the wider community have been shared by many settlers. For Shashi Dholakia, some people's failure to learn the host language held back initial integration, but there were other problems too: "Obviously you need to have a grasp of, basic understanding of the language, that was one reason, but I found the community here was very conservative with a little 'c' and they were looking after themselves, not really sort of mixing with people and that I found very, very strange. Coming from India where... you mix into a crowd and you know you can talk to anybody and everybody will talk to you."

Farhat Lateef comments that she has noticed that the Pakistani community continue to practise their religion as they did when they first arrived here. In Pakistan, "they are changing with the world but we are still keeping those traditions alive in ourselves".

The South Asian Community Today

Jamila Amar reflects upon how attitudes have changed since her arrival thirty years ago: "When I came in I saw quite a few times some silly people once or twice say 'oh you can smell the curry', but now you find the all the white people going into these shops to buy and eat curry. I had English neighbours on both sides who were so good. When my husband used to be on nights, she used to tell me that 'if something happens, you just have to knock on the wall and my husband will be there in a minute'. She was like my real sister. Over the years people have built relationships. The Asians who have come into Northampton have adjusted themselves you see. In the beginning when people came here they wanted to keep up with their own culture only, but now they've kept some of their culture but they have adopted the English culture which doesn't make it very difficult for the English to accept them."

Sarwat Khakhar is more forthright, as she looks back upon her own changed attitudes towards equality and cultural difference: "We've learnt to stand up for ourselves, whereas I think if you asked me thirty years ago, I may not be able to say things what I can say now. It's because I'm confident to say 'Yes - this is my right'."

Britain has a long history of absorbing newcomers who have brought with them their rich and diverse cultures. The great migration of South Asians to Britain since 1948 has had a major impact on British society. However social tensions persist in some parts of the country, and the debate over "assimilation" and "integration" still continues.

It is probably safe to say that the conclusions of

Dancing to Bhangra music

national surveys are reflected locally. Some South Asians have a distinctive flair for entrepreneurship, and many businesses set up in the early days continue to flourish. South Asian people often hold a degree or its equivalent, and continue to have a significant presence in the medical professions. However, they are still under-represented in the fields of law, teaching, the civil service, and the media. South Asian people still suffer from a higher-than-average rate of unemployment and Pakistanis and Bangladeshis, often from a rural background, have fared less well educationally than other population groups. Many elements of South Asia's rich and diverse cultures, particularly the culinary, have been enthusiastically adopted by British society. A recent poll found that chicken tikka masala has surpassed fish and chips as the nation's favourite dish. Northamptonshire's *Yellow Pages* list nearly a hundred "Indian" restaurants (mostly run by Bangladeshis). Bhangra music is increasingly popular. The popularity of Northamptonshire and England spin bowler Monty Panesar shows how a sportsman with a strong South Asian cultural identity, who sports a beard and turban and extols his Sikh faith, can nowadays be readily accepted and admired as a local and national role model.

Monty Panesar

Further Reading:

S. Allen, *New Minorities, Old Conflicts* (New York: Random House, 1971)

N. Deakin, *Colour, Citizenship and British Society* (London: Panther Books, 1970)

P. Fryer, *Staying Power* (London: Pluto Press, 1984)

C. Hill, *Immigration and Integration* (Oxford: Pergamon Press, 1970)

D. Hiro, *Black British, White British* (Bristol: Eyre and Spottiswoode, 1971)

C. Holmes, *John Bull's Island: Immigration and British Society* (London: Macmillan, 1988)

S. Lahiri, *Indians in Britain* (London: Frank Cass, 2000)

R. Visram, *Asians in Britain: 400 Years of History* (London: Pluto Press, 2002)

See also R. Alcock, 'Post-war settlement from the Indian subcontinent: local experience and national policy', unpublished B.A. dissertation, University of Northampton, 2006 (NBHA library)

Primary Sources:

This chapter is largely based on interviews deposited in the Northamptonshire Black History Project's oral history archive at the Northamptonshire Record Office. The interviews have been transcribed and summarised and are available for reading and listening by the general public.

The Northamptonshire Black History Association's database contains some biographical information about individuals quoted in this chapter, and many others whose interviews are in the NBHP archive: www.northants-black-history.org.uk

Census statistics are available from the Northamptonshire Observatory website: www.northamptonshireobservatory.org.uk

Local newspapers include much recent information about the development of Northamptonshire's South Asian communities.

This chapter was written by Chris Pounds

African Voices

During the 1990s settlers from the African continent were often overshadowed by Northamptonshire's vibrant African Caribbean community, and the larger number of people in Wellingborough, Kettering and Northampton whose family origins lay in India, Bangladesh or Pakistan. A decade later this picture has radically altered. In the major towns, and especially in Northampton itself, African communities are steadily growing. Ghanaians, Nigerians and Kenyans have been present in small numbers for many years, but in the early twenty-first century African settlement has considerably diversified. Wars and political conflicts, as well as economic opportunities, have brought significant new communities to Northamptonshire, including Liberians, Zimbabweans and Somalis. The Northampton Somali population, in particular, is growing rapidly and becoming one of the largest Black communities in the county.

How have African families fitted into Northamptonshire life? Their experience has varied in relation to their countries of origin and reasons for coming here, and also in relation to individuals' hopes and dreams. This chapter does not attempt to reflect everyone's experience. Instead, it offers a range of personal stories and ideas from a few of the Africans who have chosen to make Northamptonshire their home.

ISMAEL ALI: New Hope for Life

Sometimes when I take a glimpse at the situation surrounding my life, I feel immensely appalled. My country is a place of great suffering: famine, war, and all the crimes that go with them. I perceive that my country is completely lacking in love and care: a nation with a deep shortage of respect, approbation and compassion. This indifference to human life has filled my heart with tremendous sadness and I have no way to relax the pain other than using my pen to share it with those who show concern for the dilemma of my country, those whose hearts still have a soft spot for humanity.

Ismael Ali

I fled Mogadishu in 2000 when I realized that staying in Somalia was no longer an option. In 1996 there was an unforgettable day when my wife and my three daughters were forced to watch as her father was slaughtered in front of her eyes. And then I was shot at the back by militia men. But it was not until 1999 that my family finally managed to find a way to escape their country's relentless violence and come to the United Kingdom.

Positively, for me, it was a nightmare. I never heard of their whereabouts for two years. It was the worst experience I could have ever imagined: fear, killing, raping and looting. I perceived massive killing. The vulnerable and the weak were at the mercy of ruthless armed militias who committed atrocities against the innocent civilians, among them children and women.

Most distressing of all is that no one was brought to justice and it does not look like they ever will be. It is high time we stood up to change the current trend of bloodshed in our country.

In the past Somalia was a land of great beauty and promise that attracted tourists from around the world, who came to enjoy the friendly people and peaceful country. Now, however, Somalia is besieged by famine, war, and violence, leaving no person unaffected. The main cause of this endless bloodshed is the Somalian tribal philosophy, which is used by cunning warlords to achieve their own needs.

My family came in the UK in June 1999 to find new life, peace and harmony. They settled in Northampton and they attuned to the new life pretty quickly, even though they experienced some difficulties in the community. They faced less obvious cultural barriers and sometimes heard derogatory comments from cynical people, saying 'You asylum seekers, scroungers, benefit frauders' and so on. Subsequently there was tension, but that ceased when they integrated very well in their new society.

Furthermore, I too adjusted to the new environment. Firstly it was pretty daunting because of going from the unknown to the unknown. As a community activist and educator, I have worked to bridge the cultural and practical gaps between the Somali community and the wider community. I helped to create the Northamptonshire Somali community. I had to make new friends and adapt to a different life style, and also learn to live in a multicultural society that, I have to say, is full of empathy and stamina.

It is almost seven years since we left our beloved country, but we now consider Northampton as home and believe that we have learned a lot and there is a lot still to be learned. The Black History Project has made it possible for us that our voices are heard.

As a result of the integration, I am proud that my wife and three daughters have made enormous achievements. My wife has done English and dress-making courses. My eldest daughter has graduated from the University of Loughborough. We are hoping that the second will finish University in 2008 and, last but not least, the third one is studying Child Care at the Northampton College.

Substantial numbers of Somalis managed to come to the UK in the late 1980s and early 1990s. Most of them are working and contributing something to their new country. We all believe that all human beings are created by one God and are equal. No White is better than Black, and vice versa.
Currently I am working with my new organization, the Somali Health Awareness Foundation, which aims to raise health awareness in the community. I hope that we will come together and build a safe, healthy United Kingdom with full enthusiasm and happiness.

John Brownell

JOHN BROWNELL: Liberia

After the struggle for liberty in the American Revolution, free and enslaved African Americans faced continued hardship and inequality. Some voices called for the return of African Americans to the land of their forebears, leading to the founding of Liberia in 1822. Liberia is located on the West Coast of Africa and got her independence as the first Republic on the continent of Africa on 27 July 1847.

A military coup led by Samuel K. Doe, an indigenous Liberian, on 12 April 1980, overthrew the government that had held sway over Liberia since 1847. This ended Liberia's first Republic. Charles Taylor, an American-Liberian, and his followers toppled the Doe-led government in 1990. This action helped to precipitate a civil war. Various ethnic factions fought for control of the nation.

The earliest group of Liberians known to have settled in the United Kingdom were from the Kru tribe, who were predominantly seamen in the early 1920s. They settled in Liverpool.

Liberians in the United Kingdom have settled here for different reasons: some came here for academic studies and could not return home due to the civil war; some are asylum seekers fleeing the war; others settled here due to marriage to British citizens who worked in Liberia before the civil war; and lastly, others came here under the Gateway Protection Programme of the Home Office.

On 19 April 2003, Liberians in Britain met in Northampton to unite and form an organisation that would provide a range of services and activities for Liberians living in the United Kingdom and those brothers and sisters internally displaced in Liberia and also in refugee camps in Africa. We thought of the need to work with the various communities in improving their living conditions through education, advice, information, volunteering and counselling. We have regular meetings and cultural performances to teach the kids born in Britain about the rich cultural heritage of Liberia. The founder and chairman is myself, John Nimly Brownell of Northampton.

During the last few years, Liberians from all over the United Kingdom felt the need to establish an umbrella organisation of all the Liberian associations/organisations in the United Kingdom. After many meetings around the country and much hard work, the Union of Liberian Organizations in the United Kingdom (ULO-UK) was finally formed on the 25 November 2006, at the first Annual General Meeting held in Birmingham.

Liberians are very friendly people and will always make you laugh and treat you as if you have known each other for years, even if it is your first-time meeting. Our culture is based on respect for older people and the customs are similar to those of

Liberian dancers in Northampton

the United States. There are fifteen political sub-divisions of the country and seventeen tribal groups. English is the primary language. There are traditional laws and customs of the indigenous people that are respected and observed. The staple food in Liberia is rice.

Austin Madu

AUSTIN MADU: Journey to the Unknown

I left Nigeria for further studies in the United Kingdom on 23 December 1971. I was met at the airport by my brother's wife. This was the beginning of winter. Everywhere around me looked so bright that the night counterfeited the day. Travelling on the underground system was an exciting moment. I travelled from London to Liverpool to be with the rest of the family.

While in the taxi from Lime Street Liverpool, I saw a group of white men emptying the refuse bin. I had to look closely to make sure that I was not dreaming. In Nigeria we were not told that a white man could be employed as a labourer. This was a shock to me. By midday the clouds were gathering and soon darkness fell. At first I thought I had just witnessed the eclipse of the sun, but was soon put right that in winter the nights are longer than the days. I soon fell asleep. I woke up several times hoping to see the sun rise from the east, but was greeted by complete darkness outside. For the first few days I could not tell when it was morning or night.

On 3 January 1972 I arrived in Northampton from Liverpool to enrol at the College of Technology for my A-level course. When I went to the College canteen for lunch, the soup of the day was "chicken soup". My great expectation of having chicken soup was dashed when the soup contained no chunks of chicken, as it would if served in a canteen in Nigeria. Needless to say, I held up the queue for a while in the hope of getting some chunks of chicken. If the menu says oxtail soup in Nigeria you get pieces of oxtail when served, but not so in England.

Another embarrassing moment was when I was directed by the accommodation officer to a landlord. She said, "The landlord is a coloured man". On arrival, I pressed the door bell, and out came this Black man. I apologised profusely to him that I had come to the wrong house, thinking that the dignified expression for Whites in England is the word "coloured". After all, I had only been in the country for less than three weeks.

As an African, I never walked past anyone without saying "Good morning" to them in the street, but this gesture was often met with complete silence and strange looks. I was later told that it is not customary to greet anyone in the street as we do in Nigeria.

Saturday Market in Northampton

Go wherever you may go, no place like home!

VICTOR UKAEGBU: Northampton, a Barometer for Cultural Integration

Nothing teaches a people or society more about themselves, and life in general, than history; yet history's experiences are all too frequently, jettisoned as peoples and societies develop in new directions. This is why, despite the undeniable evidence of the human degradations that scarred the world on account of the Transatlantic Slave Trade from Africa to Europe and America, the later Jewish Holocaust of the Second World War, and the numerous national and ethnic conflagrations that the world has witnessed since then, some people still manage to ignore the effects of these catastrophic events in a constantly changing socio-cultural landscape. The insensitivity to inevitable changes in global demographics has all too often led to racial intolerance, to anti-immigration and anti-asylum legislation. These measures impact on the movement of peoples across the globe taking place for any number of reasons: from escaping from war, genocide and famine, to the search for new horizons and economic advancements.

Immigration figures prominently in societal transformations and has always been part of mankind's evolution, but rarely has it deserved the kind of interest it has generated since the last decade of the twentieth century. Northampton has, in many respects, been part of the reconfiguration of the British cultural landscape and I, like other past and present immigrants, have been part of that development.

I came here from Devon on 1 November 1997, but settling in Northampton has been part of a life of immigration. This began way back in my native Nigeria, but took on a different dimension when I left in 1992 to continue my education in the UK. This is the case with most immigrants from Nigeria, who generally come to the UK for education, for business, because of historical links between the UK and its former colonies, and to join families in the Diaspora. I am one of a majority of Nigerian immigrants drawn to Northampton on account of my life-long involvement in education. My decision to settle in Northampton was very challenging, the most daunting being the distance, the longing for the familiar, and the sometimes traumatic personal sacrifices which most people face whilst loosening their ties to the past and sinking new roots in a different society and culture. Overcoming these challenges was as hard as the weather was cold. But without being conscious of it, I was soon becoming part of a multicultural Northampton whose many facets are still unfolding.

Victor Ukaegbu

Since then, I have witnessed the steady evolution of Northampton into a cultural melting pot including peoples from every corner of the world: Asia, Africa, the Caribbean, North America, and most recently from Central and Eastern Europe. The population now best-described as Nigerian-British, that resides in this town, has grown as have other African and Asian societies. From one collective Black community, there are now many. This is the strength of the town and the county of Northamptonshire. The co-habitation of many groups in relative harmony is not to deny the presence of racial tensions and actual racist incidents in isolated pockets. There is still the unfortunate labelling of people either as asylum seekers or economic migrants, and cases of outright discrimination by people across all races and cultures. Despite these, Northampton is a better, richer place and is what it is, on account of immigration. My personal experience of Northampton is of a town with a warm and friendly heart, in which every community and cultural expression is celebrated and valued. This is the image of the town that the council and all sections of Northampton have held up to the world: this is the condition that will continue to shape the future of the town and county.

I have seen Northampton grow into a more diverse community, its various sections represented in every sphere including business, education, politics, industry and commerce. The stability of the town derives from a common desire by all sections to live in harmony. Political stability and cultural harmony are rare assets and are due to the steady, though sometimes frosty, integration of new settlers. I believe that there is every need for the entire community to nurture racial and cultural cohesion, and to stand together in unity against all forms of intolerance and bigotry. Although I speak for myself here, I believe I reflect the sentiment of many Nigerian-born immigrants and Nigerian-British citizens in saying that Northampton, like nearby, much-more-cosmopolitan London and similar towns and cities throughout the UK and beyond, is fast becoming "a home from home".

LETICIA NARH: We Have Settled in Northampton, But Are Our Children Happy?

Ghana is a Christian country located along the west coast of south Saharan Africa, with over a hundred ethnic groups. In the last twenty years Ghanaians have migrated into different countries of the world and the United Kingdom is no exception.

Most Ghanaians started to settle in Northampton in the last ten years, but before then a handful of Ghanaians lived here and made their mark here through the Ghana Union, long before some of us. When we came, there were a few Ghanaians at the University of Northampton and a couple of them were nurses in the community.

Ghana Union Durbar, Northampton

Five years after I moved to Northampton, I relocated to Rectory Farm. I came home within days of moving into my new home to find it broken into through the downstairs window. Although nothing was stolen, the thought of somebody coming into my home and touching things was very unsettling. The police suspected a "one-off" game by the teenagers and assured me of a Neighbourhood Watch.

However, even after many months they kept throwing eggs at my windows. My next-door neighbour, the only foreigner I have seen on my street so far, told me how she is being terrorised by the teenagers in the area. Her barn was burnt, her car window smashed, her plants turned over and her window broken at one time. I wondered if they did not want a Black family near them. I was so scared, but I needed to be strong for my children.

Though I was a Junior Secondary School teacher in Ghana, I have shamelessly feared teenagers in this country. I suspect they are impulsive and without any particular sense of responsibility and direction. On the other hand I feel they are marginalised and isolated, and the only way to make their presence felt is to challenge each other to seemingly unacceptable social behaviours, hence the thoughtless games they seem to embark on.

In the last few years there have been growing reports of knife crime, gun culture, slapping people and recording it on their mobile phones and so on, especially in our big cities such as London, Birmingham and Nottingham. Northampton is gradually growing, and I wonder if there is anything one could do to make teenagers more accepted in this society.

I found myself talking to some of them hanging around my area. My children wanted to play outside and I wanted to know who was there to play with. They seemed very innocent, wanting to know how we were settling in, and they genuinely sounded extremely pleasant, uncomplicated and even concerned. I never mentioned the egg-throwing and the break-in, but I suspected they already knew all about it. I started observing some of the teenagers in my church and I felt the need to talk to them. In fact, it was as if they only came to church because their parents expected them to be there. I decided to get them talking about their life in general and how different or similar it is to life in Ghana, since most of them have either been to Ghana before or were born there or lived elsewhere in the United Kingdom. I sat back and watched them discuss the topic at hand.

They sat in the round, which was typically Ghanaian, but with an attitude of unconcern. Yet each contributed actively to the discussion at hand. Some of them were playing with their phones, whilst others bounced a football around. I only interfered to keep the discussion on the right track. I was not there to judge them, and so discouraged all the parents who overhead them and tried to get them to sit up properly and reconsider what they were saying. I noticed how different they were from our generation: they acted and spoke differently, they seem more open about the way they felt, and they seem very respectful. They addressed me as "Auntie" and spoke very humbly. They seem like a freedom-loving generation. Some of them said "We did not ask to be born", and complained that Ghanaian parents are over-protective and so the children are not given the freedom to do as they please. But then, I thought to myself, "How free can one be in this life?".

There was a mutual agreement on how they were perceived by adults in this society. Lennox said, "The sighting of a group of Black youth puts fear in people"; he went on to say that there were times when corner shops, especially, are deserted as soon as two or three Black boys enter. The group agreed that they feel uneasy when people look over their shoulders and steal glances at them, as if they are trouble-makers. Sometimes only one or two of them are allowed into a shop at a time. Kojo said, "Life is easier in the UK, but we feel more accepted in London than in Northampton".

On the issue of respect and discipline, Mildred and Enoch agreed emphatically that the youth of Ghana is more respectful. Jurgen argued that it is because one is disciplined by all in the community. At this point, the group was completely divided on what is considered acceptable and unacceptable discipline. Some pointed out that, due to certain forms of punishment, children pretend to be respectful out of fear. Others said Ghanaian parents treat their children like "slaves": they expect their children to "clean after them", do their washing, iron their clothes, as well as do other household chores. To some of them, this was unacceptable. Some of them, especially the girls in the group, disagreed and explained that they feel the need to help their hard-working parents.

I found the argument very alarming, and our teenagers very vulnerable to serious cultural conflict. How could they reconcile their obligations to their parents with the accepted way of life in this country, where human rights and the law seem to overtake the parent's judgement? In Ghana the saying "Ga 'ma kwe bo ni o gye nyanyoo koni o kwe me ni ndaa a faamoo", literally meaning "I will cater for you while your teeth grow so that you cater for me when I start to lose mine", is acceptable in every tribe almost as the very core of our existence. If values such as this wise saying - "Ga 'mo kome foo she dzeee mo kome kweo le" ("It takes a person to give birth but a community to bring up a child") – are not instilled in our children, as it was in us, are we not becoming alien to each other's cultures?

The young people expressed an inability to feel a part of the society in Northampton, as they did in London. They explained that in London it is easier to be comfortable in their skin, because it is more multicultural and they get on better with teenagers of other cultures. Lennox and Daniel said, "In Ghana you are expected to achieve more in school, to be accepted or portrayed as popular". They all agreed that you need to be an intelligent and studious student in order to be respected in schools in Ghana, whereas in the UK you must be strong, aggressive, popular and good at sports. Northampton, as they put it, "limits us to the Black youth because we seem to

Leticia Narh with her family

be feared more and British parents especially protect their children from us".

Most of us moved to Northampton for better job prospects, to be near friends and families, and to protect our children from the rising crime in London. We have settled quite well here. When I first came to Northampton there was no Ghanaian shop. Now there are about four such shops in Northampton: Markola and Nana on the Wellingborough road, Asafo market on the Kettering road, and Kaneshie market in Far Cotton. There are now about six Ghanaian hairdressing saloons, and a couple of independent hairdressers who work from home.

There is no Ghanaian food that you cannot find in Northampton, no Ghanaian hairstyle that is not available, and no Ghanaian film that is not in the markets. There are more than four Ghanaian Charismatic churches here: the Victory Bible Church, Lighthouse, Christ Apostolic Church and a few others. Except for Ghana Gold and sunshine, we have comfortably settled here and we all seem very happy.

But are our children happy? As a parent, I think the joy of being among my people would be crowned by the knowledge that my children were happy as well. Therefore I ask this question: how we can make Black children happy, acceptable and confident on the streets of Northampton? But then the bigger picture would be to embrace the youth of Northampton, both Black and White, and make them more acceptable in our hope to deter antisocial behaviour in general.

This chapter was written by Ismael Ali, John Brownell, Austin Madu, Leticia Narh and Victor Ukaegbu

The Black Presence and Northamptonshire Sport
Chapter
11

Northamptonshire has a long and varied history as a sporting county. The Black people who have lived and worked in the county have followed this sporting tradition. Also many visitors have brought their own lasting and distinct styles of their sport to the county. From the late nineteenth to the mid-twentieth century, most sporting activities were undertaken as a form of leisure. However, there has always been an elite in most disciplines of sport. Following the turn of the twentieth century there was an increased interest in sporting competitions throughout Great Britain and also on an international level. With the introduction of television cameras in the 1960s, sport began to have a more far-reaching power. This chapter will examine some of Northamptonshire's Black sporting history.

Football

There has been a small group of Black footballers in the British game since the beginning of the competitive professional game in 1885. Black professional footballers are not a recent phenomenon; they existed in Britain well before the First World War.

Historically the most well-known local Black footballer is Walter Tull. He was relatively unknown nationally until 1997, when Northampton Town Football Club (the Cobblers) decided to create a memorial in his honour to celebrate his achievements both on and off the football field.

Walter Tull at Spurs

Tull is known as the first Black midfielder in Britain. Walter Daniel Tull was born in Folkestone in 1888 and, after both his parents died at an early age, he and his brother Edward were brought up in a London orphanage. However, Edward was adopted and moved to Scotland with his new family while Walter remained in London. While playing for a team in Clapton, Walter Tull's talent was noticed by Tottenham Hotspur. Tull decided to make football his profession and gave up his printing career. He started playing for Tottenham in 1909. Some members of the crowd racially abused Tull when the team travelled to Bristol City for a game. This was the first recorded time he had been subjected to overt racism in football. His game appeared to suffer, and he was dropped from the Tottenham first team after seven games.

In 1911 Tull was transferred to Northampton Town, where he became a very popular player. Tull was the first Black player to play for the Southern League. He played over a hundred first class matches and scored nine goals for the town. The club was in negotiation for his transfer to Glasgow Rangers in 1914, when the First World War broke out and Tull decided to leave his football career and join the Army. His military achievements are summarised in Chapter Seven. As the first Black combat officer in the British Army, he was a highly successful soldier until his tragic death in the last months of the War.

Walter Tull was a pioneer in both his social and sporting achievements. His visibility in the football arena and in the Army has highlighted a part of British history that is often denied. Walter Tull remains a pathfinder for all the Black footballers and Army personnel of the modern age.

In 1995 Northampton Town Football Club set up a working party to re-launch the local anti-racism in football campaign. In 1996, they became the first professional football club to adopt an Equal

Opportunities Policy. Northampton Town has been a leading supporter in the anti-racism in football campaign. The club has inspired many other teams to support the charter and campaign to remove racism from the football game. In January 1997 the official campaign to drive racism out of football, "Kick It Out", was launched at a Walter Tull Memorial Match at the Sixfields Community Stadium in Northampton. MP Bernie Grant was among the supporters who wanted to pay official tribute to this under-represented hero. In July 1999 Northampton Town Football Club erected a sculpted memorial to Walter Tull in a dedicated garden of remembrance (see the illustration in Chapter Seven).

There have since been many other campaigns to recognise Walter Tull's contribution to football and the pioneering steps that he achieved in his Army career. Northampton Town has honoured Walter Tull by naming a road after him near the Sixfields Community Stadium; the Probation Service's building in the town centre and the Student Union building at the University of Northampton have also been renamed in his honour. On 18 April 2007, Labour MP Keith Vaz presented a parliamentary motion calling for the erection of a statue in honour of Walter Tull. Campaigners in Dover, Kent, want a memorial to be raised on the cliffs of Dover because of their importance to soldiers returning from the battlefields in Europe. In Bristol, where his nephew lives, the Walter Tull Association commemorates him through educational work and a range of community achievement awards.

Other Black footballers soon followed the sporting career path which Walter Tull had helped to open up. Between the World Wars, in 1938, Northampton Town Football Club signed John Parris as a winger. This signing made Parris the first Black player to play national League football for Northampton. He appeared twenty-six times and scored seven goals. Parris later went on to become the second Black player to represent any of the British national sides when he played for Wales in 1932. (In the 1870s and 1880s Andrew Watson, the first Black international, played for Queen's Park, Glasgow and also captained the Scotland team in international football games.) Parris was born in Chepstow, Wales, in 1911. He was with Northampton Town Football Club from November 1937 until June 1939. Parris also played for Bradford (1928-1934), for Bournemouth (1934-1936) and for Luton (1936-1937).

Beginning in 2004, the Northamptonshire Black History Project ran a series of projects in conjunction with the Northampton Town Football Club and the Local Education Authority. The football, racism and cultural heritage projects in local primary and supplementary schools linked the stories of local Black historical figures to sport, as they explored themes of identity, accomplishment, discrimination and exclusion. The outcomes, including paintings, pottery, poems and play scripts, were displayed at the football stadium in December 2004.

This scheme led to the Race 2 Score project that has encouraged learning about Northamptonshire's diverse history through workshops, history, drama and visits to heritage organisations. Pupils from secondary schools in Corby and Northampton worked for a year developing their understanding of racism and its effects. They discovered the history of Black people's contribution to society, and in particular to Northamptonshire life. In July 2006 and March 2007, young people from the Race 2 Score project performed a play entitled *Black or White, who cares ... it's just a colour.* This play celebrated a hundred years of diversity in Northamptonshire. In 2008 Race 2 Score launched a film club, developing new skills as well as finding new ways of recording local history.

The Cobblers have had a number of Black players join their ranks since Tull and Parris. From 1972-78 Northampton-born Paul Stratford was in the team, although his promising career was plagued by injuries; from 1975-78 there was Derrick Christie; in 1978 Neil Cordice joined for one year. Other Black players have included: 1982–84, David Syrett; 1983-85, Wellingborough-born Frankie Belfon; 1984-87, Ian Benjamin (NTFC Player of the Year in 1987);1984-85, both Trevor Lee and Northampton-born Stephen Brown; 1986-89, Glenville Donegal; 1986-89, Keith McPherson (NTFC Player of the Year in 1990); 1989-91, D. Johnson; 1988-92, Trevor Quow (who later became a Professional Footballer's

Association representative); 1989-93, Steve Brown; 1990-93, Terry Angus; 1993-94, Terry Fleming; 1995-97, Jason White; 1995-96, Jason Beckford; 1994-97, Garry Thompson (who joined the coaching staff in 1996); 2005-07, Ian Taylor; 2005-07, Jerome Watt; 2001-04, Derek Asamoah; 2002-03, Armand One.

Northampton Town Football Club, 1989 squad

Cricket

From 1860 to 1865 the Racecourse Ground Promenade was the home of Northamptonshire cricket, but the Northamptonshire team always had to fight to use the 130 yards of turf for cricket. The owners of the land, the Freemen of Northampton Borough, had an ongoing disagreement with the cricketers over the use of the land. In 1885 the county moved to their current home base at the County Ground in Wantage Road. The County Ground was built to accommodate several sports; it had facilities for lawn tennis, athletics and bowls, and there was also a cycle track. From 1897, football was also played at the County Ground.

The earliest overseas cricketing visitors are recorded in 1886, when the Parsees became the first sportsmen from India to tour England. They returned for a second tour in 1888. The Parsees, originally from Persia, became pioneers of the game of cricket in India, as they were the first local community to take up cricket. During their first tour, in July 1886, the Parsees visited Northamptonshire and played a match at the County Ground against the Northamptonshire Gentlemen. The county team won by an innings and 62 runs. The *Daily Record* reported that a victory had been "generally anticipated". The Parsees had "made but a sorry stand" in their first innings, and they "seem to lack that patience necessary to play a slow head bowler", as well as lacking "that quickness of eye necessary to a finished bat". However the result was reversed in July 1888, when the Parsees won the match by 97 runs.

Parsee cricketers in Britain, 1880s

In August 1906, as part of their first tour of England, the West Indies cricket team played a three-day match in Northamptonshire. The West Indies won by 155 runs. Lebrun Samuel Constantine (father of Learie Nicholas Constantine, Britain's first Black peer) was a member of the team that visited the county. Other notable visiting cricketers in that team were George Challenor (the first West Indian to score 5,000 first class runs), and Percy Goodman (one of the first great West Indian batsmen).

The West Indies team visited Northamptonshire on several other occasions. In 1923 the visiting team managed a match draw with Northamptonshire. Five years later, at a three-day match in June 1928, the West Indies team were victorious by an innings and 126 runs. Learie Nicholas Constantine scored 107 runs and took seven wickets in the first innings, taking a further six wickets in the second innings. Learie Constantine was the great Trinidadian all-rounder who gained unprecedented fame in England due to his cricketing skills, especially during his time in the Lancashire League. The 1933 and 1966 matches at the County Ground resulted in Northamptonshire victories by an innings and 62 runs in 1933 and four wickets in July 1966. Garfield Sobers was a member of the visiting West Indies team in 1966. On a national level, the West Indies touring team beat England by three matches to one. However, the local victory run continued in May 1969, when the guest West Indies team was beaten by 65 runs. West Indian international Trinidadian Donald Ramsamooj came to Northampton in 1957; he spent three years qualifying then joined the full county team in 1960.

The international India team also visited the county regularly. They were in Northampton in 1911 for part of the first Indian tour of England, in Kettering in 1932, again in Northampton in 1936, 1946, 1952, 1967, 1982 and 1986. While in Northampton during the 1946 tour of England, the Indian team were held to a draw in a three-day match. This result came immediately after England had beaten India by ten wickets in the First Test at Lords.

Bangladeshi cricket supporters in Northampton

Raman Subba Row was the fourth cricketer of Indian origin to play for England. He made his test debut in 1958 against New Zealand and played a total of thirteen Tests for England. His father had travelled from India to study law at Dublin University. After moving to England, Subba Row's father met and married an English woman who was to be his mother. As a young man Raman Subba Row did two years' national service with the Royal Air Force. He played against India in 1959 at the Oval, when he scored 94 runs.

Subba Row joined the Northamptonshire County Cricket Club in 1955. He played first class cricket for ten years until his retirement in 1961. Subba Row jointly holds two top ten club records, for the best partnership for the sixth and ninth wickets. In 1958 he scored 376 at the Oval with Albert Lightfoot, and in 1955 scored 155 with Sydney Starkie. In 1955 Subba Row achieved the individual record of scoring the county's highest ever innings, 260 not out. He broke his own record by scoring 300 against Surrey in 1958.

Subba Row was Northamptonshire team captain from 1958 to 1961, and in 1961 he was named Wisden Cricketer of the Year. This was the same year he retired from cricket to go into business. The *Northampton Independent* lamented his departure, as "a young man who, probably even now, has not reached his peak form...he has played some magnificent innings". But he did not entirely leave the cricketing world. From 1974-78 he was chairman of Surrey County Cricket Club, and he was also an influential member at Lords, as well as a member of the Test and County Cricket Board from 1987-90. Subba Row eventually became better known as a Test match and One Day International match referee than as a cricketer, positions he has held since 1991.

Northamptonshire County Cricket Club has had many outstanding overseas players, such as Bishan Bedi (1972-77), Roger Harper (1985-87), Winston Davis (1987-90), Curtly Ambrose (1989-96), Kapil Dev, Mushtaq Mohammad (1965-77), Anil Kumble (1995), Devon Malcolm (1998-2000) and Sarfraz Nawaz (1969-82). Mushtaq Mohammad scored more than 1,000 in every season that he was with the club. He scored 72 hundreds in a first class career that spanned 502 games. His many records include a highest county score of 303 not out. He was the captain of Northamptonshire between 1975 and 1977, and in 1976 led the team to their first-ever national trophy when they were victorious in the Gillette Cup. They also equalled their highest position in the County Championship when they were placed second in 1976.

Many of Northamptonshire's Black cricketers have achieved the honour of being named Wisden Cricketer of the Year: Mohammad (1963); Dev (1983); Ambrose (1992); Malcolm (1995); Kumble (1996); Monty Panesar (2007). Kapil Dev was also named Wisden's Indian Cricketer of the Century in 2002. Other talent in the Northamptonshire side has included Pakistan-born England international Uzman Afzaal and the young competence of Mark Nelson, who has played for the England Under–19 team and won the 2006 Denis Compton Award for the "most promising young player".

There has also been cricketing passion at a local non-professional level, as illustrated by the commitment of Carl McFarlane. McFarlane was used to playing cricket from the time he was a young boy in Jamaica and he carried his passion for the game with him when he migrated to England in 1973: he arrived in Northampton on a Friday and was playing cricket as a member of the United Social Club the very next day! McFarlane has three brothers who were also cricketers with the United Social Club One of his siblings, Les McFarlane, was selected for the local county side to play first class cricket. Other members of the team included Garfield Liburd, Josh Barnett, Volt Cameron, Bunny McFarlane, Dudley and Charlie Brown. The Northamptonshire County Cricket Club's centenary history noted in 1986 that the "United Social Club [was] playing exciting cricket".

The United Social Club cricket team, formed in 1963, was affiliated to the Northampton Cricket League from 1965 and they played their local matches on the Racecourse. They would travel all around the country, for example to Bristol, Manchester and Birmingham, to compete. In 1977 the team won their first trophy in the League and they repeated this success for nine successive years. As the centenary history put it, the club was "instantly successful. Playing entertaining and forceful cricket, the side made steady progress and ... won the championship in their first year of entry!" In their first twenty-nine years as members of the League, the United Social Club team went on to win the trophy twenty times. They have also been repeated winners of the local Garnet Cup trophy. This success has been wholly due to the passion and excellence of the players and management. Carl McFarlane also played cricket for the Derby County League and for Lancashire. He has used his knowledge of the game to encourage and coach youngsters who are new to cricket.

Boxing, wrestling and weight-lifting

Larry Gains was a popular Black Canadian boxer who was in Europe from 1927 to 1930. He was a professional boxer from 1923 until 1941. His first visit to England was in the year he turned professional. On a subsequent visit he spent time living, training and working in Desborough, Northamptonshire. He lived locally with his German wife and their two children, Harold and Otty. Gains trained both in Desborough and in Northampton. However, following a fight with Phil Scott, heavyweight champion of Britain, and after receiving financial incentives, he moved to Leicester to continue his career. The *Northampton Daily Chronicle* newspaper reported in 1931 that: "Gains has had a house and a motor car presented to him by sporting admirers. Such are merely the lesser advantages to be derived from being able to punch. To receive £2,000 for four minutes sparring without receiving a single blow, as Gains did on Saturday, shows the ridiculous extremes we have reached today in the relation of services rendered."

Larry Gains and his family

Gains remained popular in Northamptonshire, and in 1933 he was "heartily toasted at a complimentary dinner" when he returned as Heavyweight Champion of the British Empire. Gains used his popularity to gain support for the Northampton hospital when he attended the hospital parade and carnival in Abington Park in June 1933. He was British Heavyweight Champion between 1931 and 1934 and he was also Canadian Heavyweight Champion. Gains returned to Northamptonshire in the 1970s to promote his autobiography, *The Impossible Dream*. He died in Cologne, Germany, in 1983. In 1994,

Gains' boxing history was part of an exhibition in the Market Harborough Museum which included details of his time in Northamptonshire.

In October 1984, the *Chronicle and Echo* newspaper ran an article headed: "Black Roots Go Deep Into County's Past". The article gave, amongst other things, details of local Nigerian boxer Jim Maloney (also known as Sidney Harcourt Maloney). The fighter had regular bouts in London and the surrounding areas. Maloney appeared at the County Ground several times in 1932-33. His arrival in Northampton was a mistake, as he had been heading to Nottingham for a fight. However, following his warm welcome to the town, he decided to stay and soon married a local girl, sister of two boxers. In the 1930s Jim Maloney and another local boxer, Joe Mitchell, took part in an exhibition fight at Althorp House; the fight was arranged because the incumbent Earl had never seen a boxing match. Maloney's friend and biographer Cyril Green recalled that he put on "a spirited exhibition". Jim Maloney died in Creaton hospital in October 1970 and was cremated at Milton Malsor Crematorium.

Boxers from all parts of the world have visited Northampton for exhibition fights and shows. In 1914, at a time of severe unrest in the county, there were newspaper reports of fighting between farmers and labourers. For protection, farmer Mr Whitehead brought in "Black Boxer Jim Johnson described as a massive nigger and cousin of Jack Johnson".

The first Black heavyweight boxing champion of the world, Jack Johnson, was a visitor to Northamptonshire at the beginning of the twentieth century. In 1916 Johnson and his wife appeared in the revue *Seconds Out* at the Palace of Varieties in Gold Street, Northampton. This was his first appearance as an actor. Large crowds of people waited for over an hour to see the world champion boxer. While in the town Johnson also staged a three-round exhibition boxing match with local man Bob Hayes, which delighted the spectators.

Jack Johnson fighting in America

After leaving the county Jack Johnson headed to London to continue his journey out of the country to South America as the Government, under the Aliens' Restrictions Act of 1914, had decided to expel him from England. Jack Johnson's world championship title fight in 1910 against white American Jim Jeffries had caused race riots in America, and films of his victories over white fighters were banned in Texas. In 1932 Black American Flutey Green was evenly matched against Charlie Taylor from Northampton at the Rivoli Skating Rink in St James. 1933 saw Black Welshman Cuthbert Taylor beat local man Harry Brown as they fought at the Drill Hall to raise funds for the Mayor's Distress Fund. The *Northampton Independent* newspaper showed an action photograph of Black fighters Sonny Osemegie and Nat Jacobs when they met in the Drill Hall in 1961.

Wrestling has always attracted large crowds of supporters. In 1933 the *Northampton Mercury* reported that a West Indian known as "Black Butcher Johnson, a coloured man" drew a six-round middle-weight match with Billy Woods of London. However, a subsequent bout had Johnson acting as peacemaker when the competitors started fighting outside of the ring in the Fanciers' Club, Wood Street, Northampton. This event was reported by the *Mercury* under the dramatic headline "Wild Scene at Northampton. Competitors Fall to the Ringside Seats. Event Abandoned".

Another notable resident of Northampton was the Black South African weightlifter Precious McKenzie, who lived in the town in the 1970s. He had migrated to England when his country refused to pick him for the 1958 Empire Games because of its apartheid policy. McKenzie became a three-times British Commonwealth gold medallist weightlifter. He eventually left Northampton subsequent to redundancy from the shoe industry. He was due to emigrate to Canada following a failed British Citizenship application, but the serving Minister for Sport intervened in his case and his application was then approved. McKenzie relocated with his family to Bristol. He won a total of four gold medals, and in 1974 he was awarded the MBE by the Queen for his services to international weightlifting.

Precious McKenzie

Athletics

Local Olympian athlete Anita Doris Neil was born on the 5 April 1950. Her father was an African American soldier and her mother an English woman from Wellingborough. As a teenager Anita Neil showed talent in track and field events and became a professional athlete. In 1964 Neil attended the English Schools Athletic Association Championships in London where she won the Junior High Jump event. Following encouragement from her coach, she joined the London Olympiads Athletics Club when she was fifteen. The following year she was an international competitor at the World Championships, and one of the youngest British athletes.

In 1968 Neil was part of a team that set a new world relay record in Portsmouth. A local councillor set up a trust, the Anita Neil Athletics Fund, to assist Neil and other local athletes to compete in national and international games. In October 1968 Anita Neil travelled to Mexico City as part of the British Olympic team. She took part in the 4 x 100m relay and the 100m races. Four years later Neil was part of the Olympic team again as they competed in Munich.

At the European games in Athens in 1969 Neil won two bronze medals. On her return to Wellingborough she was greeted by officials and fans and honoured with a civic reception arranged by Wellingborough councillor Mr W.L. Perkins. Local and national newspapers reported her progress through Europe and the world. From 1968 through to 1971 Neil attended the AAA Championships for Women, where she was always placed in the first three positions in the 100m races; in 1970 she won the 100m race. Neil also successfully entered long jump events at both junior and senior levels.

Anita Neil homecoming

In April 1973 Neil attended a ceremony in London where Winston Churchill presented her with a silver commemorative medal; this was in recognition of her completing a travel scholarship created by the Winston Churchill Memorial Trust. Anita Neil has retained her love of travelling and sport. She still lives in Wellingborough, taking an active interest in fitness, and particularly in athletics.

Northamptonshire's Black sporting pioneers have played a significant part in the county's history. In earlier years their achievements included victories over the racial prejudice of sports managers and sporting audiences. Local respect and admiration followed from success on football and cricket pitches, boxing rings and athletics tracks. Nowadays professional sport in Britain, and in Northamptonshire, would be inconceivable without a host of Black sporting heroes.

Further Reading:

S. Chalke, *Guess My Story: The Life and Opinions of Leith Andrew, Cricketer* (Bath: Fairfield Books, 2003)

F. Grande, *Who's Who - The Cobblers: The Story of the Players 1920 – 1988* (London: Sporting and Leisure Press, 1988)

F. Grande, *Northampton Town F.C. The Official Centenary History* (London: Yore Publications, 1997)

A. Rand, *100 Greats: Northamptonshire County Cricket Club* (Letchworth: Tempus, 2001)

R. Ramadin, *Reimaging Britain: 500 Years of Black and Asian History* (London: Pluto Press, 1999)

V. Raiji, (1986) *India's Hambledon Men* (Bombay: Tyeby Press, 1986)

G. Sibley, *Northampton Cricket Club: A Centenary History* (Northampton: Northampton Town Cricket League, 1986)

P. Vasili, *Colouring Over the White Line* (Edinburgh: Mainstream Press, 2000)

D. Walden and J. Watson, *Northampton Town Football Club* (Letchworth: Tempus, 2000)

R. Wickens, *From Claret to Khaki* (Liverpool: Woodford Books, 2003)

D. Dabydeen, J. Gilmore and C. Jones (eds.), *Oxford Companion to Black British History* (Oxford: Oxford University Press, 2007) includes a general essay on Black contributions to British sport.

Primary Sources:
Local newspapers are a key source for local sports history, including the *Northampton Mercury, Northampton Daily Chronicle, Northampton Daily Echo, Northampton Independent and Chronicle and Echo* and a file of newspapers cuttings at Wellingborough Library. Anita Neil was interviewed by the Northamptonshire Black History Project in 2004.

The Northamptonshire Black History Association's database gives detailed references to evidence about many of the sportsmen and women mentioned in the chapter:
www.northants-black-history.org.uk

This chapter was written by Marjorie Morgan

Northamptonshire Entertained

The Black presence in Northamptonshire is shown in many areas, not least in entertainment. Individuals and groups from across the world have visited the county to entertain the public. Most of the evidence about Black entertainers comes from local newspapers and is usually just an advertisement or a review of the performance.

Northamptonshire was home to a vast number of theatres and entertainment venues during the nineteenth and early twentieth century. Northampton itself had at least three theatres at the turn of the century. The Royal Theatre and Opera House opened in Guildhall Road in 1884 and still plays host to stars of the stage. The theatre, designed by Charles Phipps, opened with a production of Shakespeare's *Twelfth Night*. Another of Shakespeare's plays was performed at one of the town's other theatres in 1831 with a young actor named Ira Aldridge taking the lead role.

Ira was born in New York in 1807 to a free Black family. His father was a preacher and had hoped that his son would follow in his footsteps, however the young Ira had different ideas. His father sent him to the African Free School which was founded by the Society for the Manumission of Slaves. Many of the future leaders of the American abolitionist movement were educated here. The school was located near to the Park Theatre and it is here that Ira probably saw his first performances. The Park Theatre hosted many English actors and English drama productions.

Ira grew a love of acting, but realising that opportunities for Black actors in America were limited he decided to travel to England. In 1824, and against his father's wishes, he boarded a boat for Liverpool. During his voyage to Liverpool Ira met the actor James Wallack.

Ira made his first appearance on the London stage in 1825. He appeared as Oroonoko in *A Slave's Revenge* at the Royal Coburg Theatre, now known as The Old Vic. He was presented to the audience as "The Celebrated Mr Keene, Tragedian of Colour". His appearance caused much attention, not least among the press. *The Times* reported that he was unable to pronounce his words properly "owing to the shape of his lips". Although there were a few positive reviews, the press was largely hostile and critical. The Act to abolish the British slave trade had been passed in 1807, but slavery was still in existence in the British colonies. There was a strong movement from the anti-slavery lobby for Parliament to abolish slavery. This was met with opposition from the pro-slavery lobby, who had strong influence among the London press.

Ira's critics were soon further agitated by his interracial marriage to a Yorkshire woman, Margaret Gill, who was nine years his senior. The negative press meant that it became difficult for Ira to secure engagements in London and so he began to travel around the country to hone

Ira Aldridge on stage

his craft. Reactions outside London were very different. Although he was still a curiosity to many, the reviews were much more positive. After his performance in *Othello* in Scarborough, he was described as an actor of genius. Othello was not the only Shakespearean role performed by Ira Aldridge. He also took on White characters such as Shylock, Macbeth and Richard III, and was praised by many of his contemporaries.

Ira Aldridge's first visit to Northampton was in 1831, when he appeared at the Northampton Theatre as Othello. The playbill describes him as "the African Roscius", an "Actor of Colour". The name Roscius was taken from the great Roman actor Quintus Roscius Gallus, who was born into slavery in 126 BC.

Ira Aldridge also appeared in Northampton in 1846. The *Northampton Mercury* advertised his performance at "the Theatre Northampton" on Tuesday 1 December, also referring to his appearance at "the Theatre Daventry" for one night only on Monday 30 November.

As in many other provincial towns outside London, the critics' reaction was mainly favourable. On 5 December the *Northampton Mercury* carried a review of his performance: "an African of colour has been playing at our theatre this week under the appellation of `The African Roscius'. We saw him as Gambia, in *The Slave*, and were agreeably surprised at the performance. His delivery is accurate, his conception good and his action is easy and dignified. While there is no lack of energy and power when the occasion requires it, he has nothing like rant or coarseness. In the scenes with Zelinda his manner was tender and pathetic. In a wider range of characters than at first would seem to be open to him, he will be a decided acquisition to the stage."

The African Roscius

Ira Aldridge as Othello

However, in London the press continued to be scathing. When Ira Aldridge returned there in 1833, the press reported that it was indecent for an actress like Miss Ellen Tree to be "pawed about on the stage by a Black man". Due to this continued negativity, Ira travelled to Europe and appeared on the stage in Brussels, Cologne, Berlin, Hamburg, Prague, Vienna, Budapest and Munich, among other places. He performed in Russia, to much critical acclaim, and became one of the highest paid actors in the country.

By the time he returned to England, Ira was loaded with honours from across Europe including the first-class Medal of Arts and Sciences from the King of Prussia, the Grand Cross of Leopold, and the Medal of Merit from the city of Berne. Chevalier Ira Aldridge, Knight of Saxony, could no longer be ignored by the London theatres, and in 1858 he performed once again in London at the Lyceum. The reaction was more positive than during his early years.

In 1863, Ira Aldridge applied for British citizenship. His first wife died in 1864 and Ira was now free to marry his Swedish opera singer mistress, with whom he had his first child, Ira Daniel, five years earlier. Ira and Amanda von Brandt had four more children, Irene Luranah Pauline, Ira Fredrick Olaff, Amanda Christina Elizabeth and Rachael Margaret Frederika, who was born shortly after Ira's death in Poland in 1867. Irene became an opera singer, Ira Fredrick a musician and composer, and Amanda an opera singer, teacher and composer. She later became a vocal coach to many actors and singers, including Earl Cameron and the young Paul Robeson when he came to Britain to play Othello.

During the nineteenth century many other Black entertainers visited Northamptonshire. Among the most famous were the Fisk Jubilee Singers, who performed to "a large, highly appreciative audience" at the Northampton Corn Exchange on 1 July 1875. This "company of ten negro minstrels" were making their second visit to Britain, for the purpose of raising funds to support a university for Black students in Nashville, Tennessee. Two years earlier they had sung for Queen Victoria. Their popularity in high society was linked to the religious nature of their "negro spiritual" songs, as well as to their direct links with the abolition of American slavery in the previous decade.

Fisk Jubilee Singers

Alongside appreciation of performances by these talented, well-trained Black singers, nineteenth century British audiences also enjoyed the crude racial stereotypes presented by "minstrels" and White actors with blacked-up faces. Northamptonshire was no exception to this trend, which continued into the second half of the twentieth century with the televised Black and White Minstrel Show. *The Slave*, in which Ira Aldridge appeared, seems to have been particularly popular in the 1830s when the abolition of slavery was being hotly debated. Playbills in the Northamptonshire Studies Collection show that it was performed at the Northampton Theatre in 1831, 1834 and 1836. It required a cast of "Mandingos" and "Foulahs" as well as "Europeans", and seems to have mixed pathos with comedy. *The Heart of an African*, also performed in 1831, was a romantic comedy which included a slave sale.

Plays and songs about the British Empire were also very popular, and often involved blacking-up by British actors representing the defeated and colonised "natives". In 1846 the Northampton Theatre presented "a new and original Oriental Drama of peculiar interest at the present time, entitled WAR with the SIKHS or BRITAIN'S TRIUMPHS IN INDIA AND THE DEATH OF SIR ROBERT SALE". This performance included "the Hero of Jallalabad" and British actors playing the parts of "Kooli, an Indoo Boy" and "Zarina, a Female Slave, Mother of Kooli".

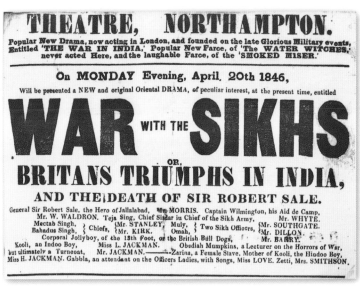
Northampton Theatre poster

Meanwhile the county continued to receive a very varied stream of visitors from different parts of the world, all eager to entertain the general public. Popular entertainment took many different forms, ranging from open-air street performance to formal theatrical events. On 14 March 1818, the *Northampton Mercury* advertised five performances at Northampton Town Hall by a troupe of Indian jugglers: "The feats of these extraordinary Indians are of the most wonderful kind, consisting of the most surprising Deceptions with Cups and Balls, changing Sand to different colours...The Performances exciting the greatest Astonishment." When real Indians were not available, British substitutes could sometimes be found. On 28 October 1836 the Northampton Theatre followed an evening drama with Mr Usher's "exact representation of those surprising performers the Indians and Chinese", including "pleasing tricks with an Egg and Handkerchief".

Indian juggler poster

The number of visiting performers multiplied as transport improved and the Empire grew. Early twentieth century newspapers present a growing number of reports showing how Northamptonshire people enjoyed "exotic" entertainments which reminded them of Britain's worldwide power. The Northampton Corn Exchange, situated on Northampton Market Square, was the venue for a famous New Zealand band on 12 June 1903. The concert was advertised in the *Northampton Mercury* as part of a Grand Military Concerts series in aid of the Union Jack Club, an organisation that supported sailors and soldiers who had fallen in recent conflicts in Africa and China. The concert was to be conducted by Lieutenant Herd, whose brother Mr W. H. Herd lived at Rothersthorpe, and the conductor had picked players and performers from all parts of New Zealand. Princess Te Rangi Pai and Maori Chief Rangi Wui were due to perform twice at 3pm and 8pm. Princess Te Rangi Pai was a stage name taken by Fanny Rose Howie (nee Porter) who was born in Tokomaru Bay in 1868. She was the eldest child of Herewaka Porourangi Potae and Colonel Thomas W. Porter, a veteran of the Maori wars. Te Rangi Pai studied singing in Australia and came to London in 1901 to continue her musical training. She toured Britain extensively, appearing at Royal Albert Hall in 1905. She also accompanied her father to Buckingham Palace when he was made a Companion of the British Empire for his services in the South African War.

Buffalo Bill's Wild West Show and Exhibition also visited Northampton in 1903. On 11 September the *Northampton Mercury* advertised the event to be staged on the Racecourse the following week. Buffalo Bill's Wild West shows toured all around Europe. The shows aimed to show "historical" scenes of how the West was won. How factually correct the scenes were is debatable. The scenes showed Native Americans attacking whites, and then Buffalo Bill or one of his colleagues riding in to save the day. The *Mercury* reported that the show had over "100 American Indians". Many Native Americans joined the show as it gave them an opportunity to travel and meet the crowned heads of Europe, including Queen Victoria. Other acts appearing at the Northampton event included the "Congress of Rough Riders of the World" and "A race of races between Cowboys, Cossacks, Mexicans, Gauchos and Indians", plus "Real Arabian Horsemen". The *Northampton Mercury* reported on 18 September that large audiences had attended both shows, with visitors travelling from miles away to witness the spectacle. The paper commented on the display of people from across the world which added to the novelty: "In the front rank were the Indian warriors in all their paint and feathers, whilst behind them were cowboys, Cossacks, Mexicans, Negroes, Arabs, Gauchos, American cavalry and last but not least, the English lancers." The long cavalcade formed as the performers departed through the town created a great stir, as many were on horseback.

Five years later a Turkish conjuror, Pasha Hayati Hassia, was drawing big audiences to the Palace Theatre of Varieties in Northampton. Described by the *Northampton Independent* as "an extraordinary human freak", he was only 39 inches high and weighed 34 pounds. His "wide and varied experience" had included learning to speak seven languages, and acting as an attendant in the Sultan of Turkey's Harem: "but on this subject he is discreet enough not to speak". Amasis the Egyptian magician paid a second visit to Northampton in 1916, having also proved very popular in the pre-war years. His performance took place at the New Theatre.

Not all visits to Northamptonshire were equally successful. In 1907 the *Wellingborough News* reported that a group of "coloured" people, natives of Dahomey, West Africa, were stranded in the town. The visitors had originally visited Wellingborough in September with a showman, and were advertised as the "fighting men and women of Dahomey". This situates them alongside many other groups of Africans brought to Britain to entertain the public with displays of "barbarism" which highlighted the benefits of imperial conquest and the

Dahomeyans stranded in Wellingborough

general superiority of the British. In London, whole "villages" of Africans were hired in for display at Alexandra Palace, and later at Olympia. However, there is some evidence from the report that the Dahomey visitors were trying to assert their independence. Interviewed by a Wellingborough journalist, they described how they had originally left Dahomey four years previously. The original group of thirteen had travelled to the Continent, exhibiting in Italy, Germany, Russia and Austria. Their visit to England was originally planned for fifteen weeks. The group opened in Leeds and went on to perform at Sadler's Wells and the Agricultural Hall. The leader of the group explained: "We wanted a white man to manage us. We got one but latterly we have only made threepence or sixpence per day. Out of that we have had to pay our expenses, the cost of the transit of our luggage, and to keep ourselves." He went on to explain that, despite this, the group managed to travel with the show to Luton, St Albans, Bedford, Rushden, Wellingborough, Kettering and Rothwell.

The show in Wellingborough took place on the Market Square at the back of the Exchange Hall. Performances were not well enough attended and after a week the showman moved the show to

Kettering; it was here that the group from Dahomey parted company from the rest of the show, and were left in the town. They managed to travel from Kettering back to Wellingborough, where at the time of the report they were residing with no means of support. The group had tried to rent a shop on a short lease, and hoped that they would be able to put on shows and earn some money. But most of the landlords wanted them to take on a lease of a year or more, which was not an option for the group. One of the group members, Felicia, said sadly: "We came to white men's country for money and we cannot go back empty. We should be laughed at."

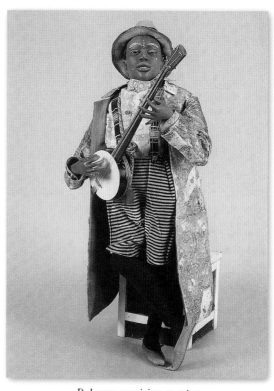

Dahomey musician as a toy

Through the sympathetic newspaper reporter's investigations, venues for the group were offered in Nottingham and Cambridge but lack of funds made it impossible for them to get there. The Dahomeyans also stated that all offers of lets were dependent on them having an Englishman with them. During the four weeks that they were stranded in Wellingborough, support and food were given to them by the Salvation Army, who eventually worked with the Wellingborough authorities to secure the group's passage to London. The Salvation Army in London was charged with finding them accommodation and trying to find them an engagement in the city.

A few years later another Northamptonshire visit ended in an even worse disaster. On 8 September 1911 the *Kettering Guardian* carried an advertisement for the "world renowned" Hadji-Mohamed Troupe's visit to the Kettering Coliseum. The following week local newspapers carried the story of

Kettering gravestone of Ali Broheim

a tragic accident to one of the troupe's members, fifteen-year-old Ali Desiri Broheim. The *Kettering Leader*, on 15 September, headed its report: "Fatal Bathe. Moorish Acrobat drowned in Kettering. Tumbler's last bathe." The article described a terrible accident in which the young boy drowned after taking a bathe in the Ise Brook on Tuesday 12 September. He had been bathing with another member of the acrobatic troupe. In the article Ali's father was described as an Arab and his mother as French. An inquest was held at the Buccleuch Hotel which recorded a verdict of accidental death. The *Kettering Leader* reported on the funeral which took place in Kettering soon afterwards: "Pathetic scenes at Kettering Cemetery. Witnessed by a large crowd...hundreds – almost thousands – gathered round the graveside". The newspaper suggested that this high turnout by the people of Kettering was due to the curiosity of witnessing unfamiliar funeral rites. Many would have been disappointed as the funeral service was that of the Roman Catholic church, the faith of his mother. Curiously, the newspaper added in the information that his father was an Arab and "evidently strict in his religion; he has never tasted pork or alcohol". Ali Broheim's grave bears an Islamic crescent.

During the twentieth century Northamptonshire people gradually became better-off and better-educated, and enjoyed an growing amount of leisure time. The entertainment industry expanded to keep up with increasing demand. For example the New Theatre opened in Abington Street, Northampton, in 1912. Locally known as the Hippodrome, it stood proudly in the space now occupied by Primarks. This large theatre played host to numerous stage stars of the day, many of them Black Americans.

Two years after its opening, American comedians Scott and Whaley appeared on the stage in Northampton. Eddie Whaley and Harry Scott came to England in 1909, initially for eight weeks, but their act was so successful that the pair never returned to America and both became British subjects. They were well known for their cross-talking act of Cuthbert and Pussyfoot which also included songs at the piano. Both men were musicians, Whaley a vocalist and Scott a jazz pianist. The pair were also the first Black performers to star in a British film. Directed by John Baxter, the 1934 film *Kentucky Minstrels* saw the duo recreate the roles they had popularised in their long-running BBC radio series. Eddie Whaley's son, Eddie Junior, later starred alongside Deborah Kerr in the 1947 film *Black Narcissus*.

In November 1932, the New Theatre welcomed the Tang Tee See Troupe from China, who were performing with Lord John Sanger's Circus Review. The following week the same review was performed in Kettering. Lord John Sanger, along with his brother George, formed one of Britain's most notable circus companies of the Victorian era. The circus name continued into the twentieth century, with tours across England.

Other visitors to the New Theatre included the American entertainers Layton and Johnstone. These two were brought into the Northamptonshire headlines by an all-star variety show in July 1933. At this point they were already well known across the world as supreme singers of syncopated songs and American ballads. The pair both had solo careers, but had met and formed their piano / vocal duo in New York in the early 1920s. In 1923 they were booked by Elsie Janis for a season in her London revue, *Elsie Janis At Home*. During their time in England, Layton and Johnstone reportedly sold over ten million records. Popular titles included "Bye-Bye, Blackbird", "River Stay 'Way From My Door", and "It Ain't a Going to Rain No More". The pair split in 1935 after Johnstone was implicated in a society divorce scandal. Johnstone returned to America, whilst Layton continued a successful solo career in London.

September 1935 saw the arrival of pianist Garland Wilson, who reportedly stopped the show with his interpretations of old and new numbers. On 20 September the *Northampton Mercury* reported: "One of the high-spots of the brilliant programme of syncopated music and variety which is being presented to crowded houses at the New Theatre this week by Jack Payne and his band is undoubtedly the brilliant playing of Negro pianist, Garland Wilson". The paper went on to describe how the impresario Jack Payne discovered Mr Wilson during a casual visit to a Parisian cabaret. Enthralled by the pianist, he invited him to tour Britain.

In November 1935 the *Northampton Independent* announced: "Hutch to visit Northampton". Theatre managers were "Fulfilling their promise to present only the very best in variety entertainment... with a visit from none other than the British gramophone and radio star". Hutch was the entertainer Leslie Hutchinson, who was born in Grenada in 1900 and came to Britain in 1924. An extremely popular cabaret singer, he was reportedly a favourite of the Prince of Wales who later became King Edward VIII. Patronised by the wealthy, he also entertained thousands in variety halls all over the country, as well as making more than four hundred recordings and seven films. During the 1930s he was reputed to be one of Britain's highest-paid performers.

Leslie Hutchinson

In 1939 the New Theatre was visited by the Peters Sisters, who were described as "rotund" on the publicity for the Harlem Double Feature *Hi de Ho / Duke Is Tops*. The three sisters, Mattye, Anne and Virginia, were born in Santa Monica and were notable for their size as well as their incredible singing voices. In his book *Cavalcade of Variety Acts 1945 -1960*, Roy Hudd remembers seeing them on the stage at the London Palladium and describes how they "stopped the show" with their wonderful singing.

Paul Robeson

West Indian soprano Alyce Fraser visited Northampton twice, performing at the Queens Road Methodist Church. On 13 and 14 February 1932 she made her first appearances at the church. The following year she returned for services on Sunday 29 and Monday 30 January. The *Northampton Independent* described her second visit as "eagerly anticipated, if only for the probability of hearing again her fine rendering of negro spirituals of which, coupled with Paul Robeson, she is one of the two finest modern interpreters."

The current Jesus Centre on Abington Square Northampton was formerly the Savoy Theatre, and in May 1960 it played host to Paul Robeson himself. By this date the legendary political activist and singer was nearing the end of a remarkable career. Born in New Jersey in 1898, as the son of an escaped slave, Robeson went on to achieve high academic and sporting honours at Rutgers College and Columbia University, before turning his talents to acting and singing. He was enormously popular in Britain from the 1920s onwards, and admired for his work to promote peace and international harmony. In America, on the other hand, he became a victim of the postwar anti-communist witch-hunt, losing his passport for a number of years. The Northampton event attracted a full house and was enthusiastically reported in the local newspaper. On 9 May 1960 the *Northampton Chronicle and Echo* described the concert and showed a photograph of the singer outside All Saints Church, smiling and chatting with a local policeman.

Inspiration FM, community radio station

It would be difficult to imagine the present-day programmes of Northamptonshire theatres without Black performers, whether actors, musicians, comedians or writers, producers and theatre technicians. Nowadays the Royal and Derngate Theatres in Northampton and the Castle Theatre in Wellingborough regularly host Black theatre companies and musical groups of every kind, and Black performers are integral to the county's entertainment scene. Clubs, pubs and street carnivals depend upon their talents, as well as professional entertainment venues. The community radio station Inspiration FM broadcasts from BBC Radio Northampton and has recently obtained its own full licence. While enjoying the diversity of the present, it is important to remember the struggles of earlier Black performers to earn the respect which they deserved, and the right to make a living from entertaining the Northamptonshire public.

Further Reading:

D. Dabydeen, J. Gilmore and C. Jones, *The Oxford Companion to Black British History* (Oxford: Oxford University Press, 2007)

R. Foulkes, *Repertory at the Royal. 65 Years of Theatre in Northampton, 1927-92* (Northampton: Northampton Repertory Players, 1992)

H. Marshall, *Ira Aldridge: the Negro Tragedian* (Washington: Howard University Press, 1993)

P. Robeson Jr., *The Undiscovered Paul Robeson: an Artist's Journey* (Chichester: John Wiley and Sons, 2001)

A.R. Tompsett, *Black Theatre in Britain* (Amsterdam: Harwood Academic Publishers, 1996)

L. Warwick and M. Toyer, *Death of a Theatre. A History of the New Theatre, Northampton* (Northampton: L Warwick, 1960)

L. Warwick, *Theatre Un-Royal* (Northampton: L. Warwick, 1974)

Information about Black entertainers is also available on many websites, including Every Generation's *100 Great Black Britons*: www.100greatblackbritons.com

Primary Sources:
The Northamptonshire Central Library has a big collection of local playbills and theatre programmes.

The local press is one of the best sources for the history of local entertainment. Detailed references to press coverage of most of the performers described in this chapter can be found in the Northamptonshire Black History Association database: www.northants-black-history.org.uk

This chapter was written by Nikki Taylor

Serving the Community

A Changing World

The presence of Black people across Britain and in Northamptonshire's public services was low until after the Second World War. Larger Black communities started to arrive in Northamptonshire and the UK in the late 1940s, while across the globe there was a sea change and Britain's empire began to erode over the following decades.

The gradual surrender of British power in India during the 1930s was followed by the partition and independence of India and Pakistan in 1947. The same period saw the growth of national independence movements in Africa, the Caribbean and the Middle East which achieved success throughout the1960s and 1970s. The business of British decolonisation was followed by the growth of American world power and its informal empire. Black people came to the UK in response to the British Colonial Office inviting Commonwealth citizens to help rebuild Britain after the war, at the same time building a more prosperous life for themselves and their families.

The arrival of the Empire Windrush, bringing settlers from the Caribbean in 1948, was followed by South Asian settlers coming to work in Britain from the 1950s, Kenyan Asian settlers in the 1960s, and Ugandan Asians expelled from Uganda by Idi Amin in the 1970s. Most people came to England with the intention to work then return home; however after settling down and having a family, many have remained in Britain to date.

People came to fill job vacancies as there was a shortage of labour after the war. Most of the new arrivals from the Caribbean went to the large towns and cities such as London and Birmingham, or to smaller towns like Northampton, to work or train in the National Health Service, the transport service and as general labour. In Wellingborough Bangladeshi workers entered the leather industry, while East African Asians found jobs in factories such as Telfers and Weetabix. The racism people faced was unexpected, because these new arrivals from the Commonwealth believed Britain was their Mother Country. The newcomers soon realised that they had been falsely reassured by Prime Minister Winston Churchill's message that they too were British.

Community Organisations and Local Government

Black communities have contributed to the post-war development of public services in Northampton, being pioneers for equal opportunities in the public services and essential to the successful delivery of much recent social policy legislation. Since the 1950s they have campaigned against discrimination and also developed their own services and businesses, as a direct result of the rejection they felt in British society and out of a need to serve their own communities. This has led to improvements for all up and down the country. It has also influenced public policy, such as the Race Relations Act of 1976, which led to the development of the Commission for Racial Equality. Community Relations Councils (CRCs) existed locally from the late 1960s onwards, and later developed into local Racial Equality Councils (RECs).

Many people who came to settle in Northamptonshire and work in public services were from the different Caribbean Islands. Some people came eventually to Northamptonshire from other towns or cities in Britain, where they had first settled. They came either directly into a training position, such as nursing for many women, or sometimes to study or to seek work with a familiar company from home. People often came to connect with a family member or a friend. Some came with the purpose of helping others, whilst other individuals stumbled into statutory or voluntary services providing education, health and social care as a response to the necessities identified in their community. New arrivals in Northampton were often not entitled to public assistance; they had to register at the labour exchange in Grafton Street to be assigned a job. The local authority services were slow to respond to the influx of newcomers, and ignorant of the needs of Black workers and their families.

People who became active in setting up various community organisations did this important work in their own free time, usually while holding down a full-time job and bringing up a family. Many of these pioneering individuals worked between local authority public services and voluntary community organisations, including mosques, temples and churches. They used their dual role to influence positive change in service provision, identifying the failure of mainstream services to meet the Black communities' needs. They resolved these issues by creating their own services from the 1950s to the 1970s, leading on to these services being amalgamated into mainstream services from the 1980s onwards. There were many individuals who were instrumental in helping to set up early Black organisations in Northamptonshire. Regrettably not all of these pioneers are featured in this chapter, due to the absence of reliable information as well as space limitations. We apologise to those people who are not mentioned here by name, and salute their achievements.

Politics

Local government is responsible for delivering many public services. In the 1940s there were no Black councillors in Northamptonshire, but as Black communities expanded some strong individuals fulfilled their ambition to serve all the people of their town or county by being elected to public office.

Stanley Liburd was born in Nevis. As a young man he was trained as a stone mason and had a keen interest in politics, touring the streets of his local parish urging people to vote for Labour. He came to live in Northampton to join friends from home. Working as an engineer grinder at RHP Bearings Ltd, he became a shop steward in the Amalgamated Union of Engineering Workers. In 1972 Stan joined the British Labour Party and in 1976 stood as a candidate in the local elections. In 1979 he became Northampton's first Black councillor for St Alban's Ward.

In 1979, in an interview with the local press, Stanley Liburd confirmed different forms of prejudice in the town, expressing concern about Black children being failed by the education system. He spoke of isolated incidents, confirmed problems between some Black youths and the police at that time and reassured readers that relationship between the West Indian community and the wider community was very good in general. He said, "I would like to see as many coloured people as possible involved in public life." His son Garfield Liburd is known locally by the Black community as Mr Motivator through his keep fit business, going round to community organizations like the African Caribbean Elders Society (ACES) and doing armchair exercises for the elderly, as well as designing sessions for individuals or groups.

Over the years the number of Black councillors has gradually increased. Jaswant

Jaswant Bains, Mayor of Northampton

Bains, a local Sikh shop keeper, was elected as councillor for Dallington ward, Northampton. He became Northampton's first Asian Mayor in 1996. Ulric Gravesande, born in Guyana and resident in Northampton since 1956, became councillor for the Delapre ward in 1987 and the town's first Caribbean Mayor in 1998. Mike Prescod, born in Barbados, served as Mayor of Wellingborough in the same year.

Chaman Kalyan was elected as councillor for Delapre ward, Northampton. In Wellingborough the first Asian councillor was Shobhi Dholakia, while Bhupendra (Bob) Patel became councillor for Hemmingwell in 2003. Meanwhile Melanie De Cruz, born in Britain in 1974, became Northampton's second Black female councillor. She followed in the footsteps of Anjona Roy, who represented the Spencer ward in Northampton whilst holding a leadership role at Dostiyo, the Northampton Asian women's organization. Later she also served as Chief Executive of the Northamptonshire Racial Equality Council (NREC).

The United Social Club (USC)

The United Social Club was the first official Caribbean organization to start in Northamptonshire in the late 1950s; it was also one of the first Black organisations in the UK. Its main function was to give people in the Caribbean community somewhere to go and socialize without being subject to racism. Over the years the USC has boasted an outstanding cricket team which has won many trophies across Northamptonshire and nationally. They also had netball and football teams, and a dominoes team which still continues its success today. They would arrange outings and activities, raise funds, hold dances, show-case performing artists and serve as a venue to the community.

Joe Dixon was born in Jamaica in 1933 and arrived in Britain in 1955. Like many early Caribbean arrivals in Northampton, he was instrumental in helping to set up the USC, working alongside Ivan Bryan, Mrs Laden, Sterling Shaw and Mr Sterling. The USC is commonly known in the Caribbean community as the West Indian Club.

Working voluntarily as a community activist, Ulric Gravesande talked about his involvement in starting up the USC in 1957 " in a room in somebody's house and subsequently we got our first premises at Regents Square and then I moved them on to the second premises". He explained how the USC became a pioneering model: "It was one of the first Afro-Caribbean Organisations to start in the Midlands; we would have people coming in, Afro-Caribbeans coming in from all over the world, all over Northamptonshire and the Midlands to see how it was run".

Ulric Gravesande has been an instrumental figure within public services in Northampton since the 1950s. He came to England to study mechanical and electrical engineering, working as an engineer for a local business for thirty years. He got his first taste of politics in Britain through work, becoming shop steward, then company union representative, then later joining the Labour Party. His many public activities have included working for the local Health Authority at St Andrews Hospital as a Mental Health Review Officer and for the Local Education Authority, supporting parents of excluded children. He served on the Council for approximately twenty years, was a magistrate for sixteen years and school governor to three schools. He supports the USC to date, and has had a leading role in the life of the organization.

Ivan Bryan, who sadly died in 1992, was also a key figure within Northampton's Caribbean community organisations. He arrived in England in 1957 and worked on the railways in London, where he first joined the union. Ivan was the first Black special constable in Northampton. In 1982 he studied youth and community work at Leicester Polytechnic, and in 1989 attended Coventry Polytechnic. Throughout all this he was one of the people that played a leading role in launching the USC and other community organisations described below.

Bert Cuff

Berston Cuff, known as Bert Cuff, was another key supporter of the USC, serving as the secretary from 1972 to 1979. He helped many Black community organisations to forge good relationships with the police. Bert moved to Northampton in the 1960s. He fought tirelessly against racial injustice, campaigned against racism and was active in many organisations across Northamptonshire both in the voluntary sector and in statutory services. He was one of the first Black social workers in Northampton in the 1980s, and in 1987 became a magistrate. The USC has clearly been the pivotal point or springboard from which other public services and other Black organizations grew.

Northampton Council of African and Caribbean Organisations (NCACO) and Northampton Afro-Caribbean Organisation (NACO)

The Northampton Council of African and Caribbean Organisations (NCACO) started in 1979. Within a week of retiring from the USC Bert became involved with Ulric Gravesande and Pasvil Plummer in setting up the NCACO.

Its main purpose was to bring together the different Black community groups under one umbrella and to educate and train the community. Bert recalls: "We felt that there was a lot of commonality in terms of ... what they did and the reason why they existed. And that would be more effective, sharing of resources." With urban aid and government funding through Manpower Services, they were able to train young people, both Black and White, in office skills, painting and decorating. They offered other organisations administrative support and access to a development officer. Bert reminisces: "at one time I had fourteen people employed in other organisations through government schemes". They developed the young people, giving them work experience through repairing the building and working in the offices. Their first premises were in Talbot Road; they then moved to Bailiff Street, and finally they acquired a building in Clare Street. The organisation lasted for approximately seven years until funding came to an end.

Some of the organisations that came under the NCACO were the Ghana Union, the Matta Fancanta Movement (MFM), the West Indian Parents Association (WIPA), the Caribbean People's Association (CPA), the African Caribbean Elders Society (ACES) and the USC. After funding came to an end those member organisations continued their independence, or served their purpose then dissolved. Members of the NCACO felt they could no longer refer to themselves as a council for other groups, so became an independent charity called the Northampton Afro-Caribbean Organisation (NACO) in the late 1980s. The NACO still survives today, serving as a community venue.

Caribbean People's Association (CPA)

The Caribbean People's Association was formed in the 1970s, and was short-lived. It was formed by people mainly living on the Eastern District, people who had moved from Birmingham and London due to the Development Corporation and growing local industry. Its focus was to establish suitable childcare provision and help settle in the newcomers. Bill Morris, General Secretary of the Transport and General Workers Union from 1991-2003, lived in Northampton at the time and was a member of the committee. After Bill moved back to London the group continued to achieve its main aims through WIPA and NCACO, and thus came to a natural end.

West Indian Parents Association (WIPA)

Morcea Walker was the driving force behind the West Indian Parents Association, together with Ivan Bryan and his wife Mavis. Born in Jamaica, she came to Northampton in 1973 as a trained teacher and worked in local schools including Northampton School for Girls. Morcea worked with others such as Ulric Gravesande, Joe Dixon, Aubrey and Gwen White and Bert Cuff. WIPA's main focus was education: it developed out of concerns from parents that Black children were being failed by the education system. WIPA began in 1974, after research by the County Council and the Community Relations Council highlighted the need for this facility.

WIPA day trip to the Isle of Wight

The WIPA supplementary school was the first project of its kind in Northampton, giving educational support to African and Caribbean children at various school locations. It was commonly known as the Saturday School in the Caribbean community. They used Stimpson Avenue School as a base, and over the years moved to Cliftonville School, then Trinity School. Mavis taught WIPA groups from its start until 2001. Speaking of her late husband's involvement, she recalled: "He used to concentrate on running the elders' day project while Mrs Walker used to concentrate on running the summer scheme and after that they started up the Saturday School." The WIPA summer play scheme, allowing parents to go to work and drop their children off safely during school holidays, was also a pioneering venture at the time.

Gwen White at WIPA Elders Project

Morcea Walker and Bert Cuff found and rented the building in Clare Street where the Northampton Afro-Caribbean Organisation is still situated today. The nursery started in 1984, and the after-school club, known as Latch Key, started in 1987. Funded from the Racial Equality Council and the Home Office, the day nursery started as a five-year project and eventually lasted nineteen years. It came to an end in 2003, as after-school facilities became commonplace across the town through expanded schools and fresh government initiatives.

The Elders Project and the African Caribbean Elders Society (ACES)

The Elders Project began in Dallington church hall in approximately 1974, from a strand of WIPA and with the help and support of leading Black community activists. Mrs Wainwright was the first co-ordinator. The Elders Service then moved to the Holy Sepulchre Church in the early 1980s. Its aim was to deliver health and care services to the elderly whose needs were not being met through mainstream services. The service users had the facilities of a drop-in service, a minibus, dominoes, bingo, Caribbean meals, day trips out and visiting speakers and performance artists. Gwen White co-ordinated the Elders Service for four years at the Holy Sepulchre Church, working hard with community support and the help of car boot sales and other fund-raisers; support was also received from the Archdeacon of Northampton.

Mavis Bryan recalls that during the 1970s Mr Bryan approached the local authority on numerous occasions, to no avail: "He went to the County Council and they weren't interested in helping Black people." Mr Bryan continued to lead the African Caribbean Elders Project until 1989 when, after much negotiation, it was taken over by Northamptonshire County Council Social Services. In 1992 the service became ACES and acquired a building on Wellingborough Road overlooking Abington Park, where they still remain today. The service users participate in various additional activities and service provision, ranging from residential, day and respite services to keep fit, educational or leisure day trips, story-telling, debates, joining in with community activities and learning new skills like information technology.

Many other local people have helped to run the Elders Project and the ACES day service, including Bert Cuff, George Cleghorn, Michael Cleghorn, Claudette Chambers and Cathy Marks. Eloise McKenzie was an early carer for the Elders Service; like other pioneers, eventually she herself enjoyed the benefits of ACES support. For many years now, Olive Robinson has been the lynchpin of ACES, earning the respect and affection of all its elderly users. Her services to the community have included publication of a wonderful collection of reminiscences by the first generation of Caribbean settlers, titled *Cold Arrival: Life in a Second Homeland* (ACES, 1998).

Wellingborough Afro-Caribbean Association (WACA)

On their arrival in Wellingborough in 1976, Mike and Joyce Prescod joined an existing Caribbean organization: the West Indian Sports and Social Club (WISSC). Joyce Prescod helped the women whose husbands had formed the WISSC to set up the Afro-Caribbean Ladies Association (ACLA), based at the Victoria Centre in Palk Road. Joyce was Secretary for the first fifteen years and Maria Mason, trained as a nurse, was Chairperson.

The Victoria Centre had provided a social base for Black American soldiers during the Second World War, and once again became a central location for Wellingborough's settled Black community in the 1970s. May Green was born in Jamaica and settled in Wellingborough. She is "the only person that is at the Victoria Centre now that's been there from (when) it started". She recalls how they acquired the derelict old church building, and how the community worked together to make it a base: "So Mike decided with Bob Bailey... that they could turn it into a community centre because there wasn't one in Wellingborough, Northampton or nowhere, where it could accept all nations."

May Green

By 1981 Mike Prescod had come up with the concept of Wellingborough Afro-Caribbean Association (WACA), embracing the idea of a holistic approach to Black community needs. They rented office space in various locations, including the Victoria Centre, before acquiring a building in Harriotts Lane to be used as an administration centre. This was the central hub of the organisation until they acquired their current premises in Rock Street in 1987. WACA obtained funding and was able to start the Afro-Caribbean Elderly Day Centre in May 1988. Juliana Hall and friends were involved in setting up a

WACA indoor bowls

new women's group which came together to arrange social events, including family fun days, sports events, evening entertainment, visiting speakers, and much more.

Brindley Walker, known as Billy Walker, and Herman Hart, who was the first Treasurer, were major players in helping to establish services at WACA. By the late 1980s WACA boasted a Saturday Supplementary School, which Billy ran for many years and which still continues today. By the 1990s they had guidance, advocacy and support services, run by Alan Howard; a Black mental health support service run by Jenny Labbon; and the lottery-funded Black Angels Project which aimed to enhance the social mobility of the Black community, headed by Norman Henry. Black and mixed parentage children's services were organised by Callum Simon and Floyd Douglas, then Carole Gardener took over until funding came to an end in the late 1990s. Despite losing major funding, WACA continues to date providing the elders' day service and a social location for the community. Lambert Hauton, Allister Charles, Margret Charles, Carole Blake, Pauline Collymore, Silvia McLauren, Clive Lesley and George Inniss are some of the original members who have worked in various positions within WACA, keeping the facility going as a service to the community.

WACA and the NACO were sister organizations. Many of the community groups which they set up and nurtured over the years were intrinsically linked because the individual community leaders consistently kept in contact with each other through Black community networks which reached across Northamptonshire and beyond.

Northamptonshire Sickle Cell and Thalassaemia Support Group

This valuable Support Group was started in 1996. The pioneers of the group, mostly with nursing backgrounds, recognised the lack of local knowledge and awareness about a blood disorder particularly prevalent in Black communities. They set about to rectify the situation.

Monica Noel was born in Grenada and came to Northampton to train as a general nurse in 1971. She later became a senior staff nurse and has been involved in the training and teaching of student nurses. She was one of five founding members of the Northamptonshire Sickle Cell and Thalassaemia Support Group, and recalls: "even the midwives, when I started they didn't know anything about sickle cell; they never did any testing or anything. We started to get the group together and we meet with the Health Authority, they now have somebody in the hospital that will talk to them." Monica remembers the voluntary fund-raising activities needed to keep the group going, including regular support from the Islanders, a group of local musicians: "putting on dances and that, they help, they have a yearly funding which

Members of the Sickle Cell Support Group

they give us the opportunity to raise funds as well." Mavis Bryan has also been an active member. In 2003 she recalled that "we got help from the County Council for three years... After that we have to find our own way by getting our own monies by keeping dances or gifts or we sell calendars in order to make money." The Group's first base was at Kettering Road, then they moved to the Billing Road premises which they shared with the Black mental health centre (Sankofa).

Janet Douglas–Hall was born in Trinidad, arrived in Britain in 1955, then moved from London to Northampton. She worked for Northamptonshire Social Services and has been involved in WACA and NACO since the 1980s: "There were a lot of Black community groups which I was really impressed with... they were doing a lot of good work". Janet has been involved in many aspects of social and health support, lending her skills and experience to community organisations such as the Women's Information and Support Centre, Sankofa mental health support, and the Northamptonshire Black History Association as well as the Sickle Cell Group. The Group continues to offer support and advice to sufferers and to raise awareness, helping families across Northamptonshire.

Black Mental Health Services

In September 1996 the Northampton African Caribbean Health and Social Care Resource Centre was officially opened in Kettering Road, Northampton, by the High Commissioner of Jamaica, Mr Derek Haven. Its aim was to deliver support and educational services to mental health sufferers and to give them a base. Bert Cuff was seconded from Social Services to become the project manager, research having proved the need for this facility: "we identified as one of our main concerns the numbers of young Black people who were being given diagnosis of suffering from mental health problems, particularly schizophrenia." The centre was run by the community and funded by the local authority under Section 11, enabling the employment of skilled, trained staff. Joan Samuel, Wendi Jarrett, Ingrid Madu, Claudette Johnson and many others worked to make the centre a success. They offered leisure and domestic activities to their users, together with drop-ins, one-to-one support, a café and educational facilities. Sadly, with cut-backs in local authority funding the project went through a forced transition. After securing some alternative funding they changed their name to Sankofa and moved to the Billing Road, Northampton. With the lease running out on the building they occupied, Sankofa's specialist services were eventually dispersed in 2006. An important community support facility was lost, despite protests from users and many other community members.

"Some doctors believe the diagnoses are wrong and that mental health problems are caused by strong feelings of alienation and even racism." Joan Samuel recognised the gaps in mental health provision for the local Black community, even while the African Caribbean Health and Social Care Resource Centre was still functioning. She galvanised extra resources, with help from family members, to set up Msaada in1998. This support centre, based further up the Kettering road from the Northampton African Caribbean Health and Social Care Resource Centre, offered dependent and independent living schemes, a restaurant, lounge, counselling and psychiatric support. In 2001 Joan's sister, Elaine Darien, was awarded the European Business Women of the Year award. Joan has been nominated as Carer of the Year for looking after young Black people with mental health issues. There is clearly a continued need for such voluntary initiatives, given the funding uncertainties which have repeatedly threatened local services in recent years.

Women in the Health Services

Black women have played a very significant role in the development of Northamptonshire's public service provision. Many new arrivals from the Caribbean in the 1960s and 1970s went directly into health services such as nursing. Some went on to develop high-level careers within the field of nursing. As we have already seen, many trained health workers also became involved in setting up pioneering community organisations.

Aubrey and Gwen White met on their journey from Jamaica to England in 1954. Aubrey, a cobbler by trade, came to Northampton hoping to start his own business, while Gwen came to Northampton to train as a nurse. They were among the first Black families to settle in Northampton after the war, and their "unusual" wedding was reported in the *Northampton Independent* beneath the heading "They Were All Jamaicans". Both were to become instrumental in helping, supporting and sustaining Black community groups in Northampton over the decades. Their daughter June Elizabeth White Smith Gulley was born in Northampton in 1957; her older brother, the late Eddie White, had been the first Black baby delivered at the Barratt Maternity Home. June moved to London to complete her training as a nurse, and was later one of the founding members of the Northamptonshire Council for Ethnic Minority Communities (CEMC), as well as a WIPA committee member and an advisor and supporter of the Northampton African Caribbean Health and Social Care Resources Centre. Her career in nursing was followed by a spell as a police officer: another "first" for the family, since she was the first African-Caribbean police officer recruited to the Northamptonshire Police Constabulary in 1978. June has also been an active member of the Northamptonshire Black History Association from the outset to the present.

Nurses from the Caribbean

Norma McFarlane was born in Jamaica and came to St Edmund's Hospital, Northampton, to train as a nurse in the early 1970s. Norma talks about the racism she experienced whilst training: "When I went into nursing at first it's not even the other nurses, sometimes the patients, they didn't want to touch you because you were Black." Cynthia Dyer, also born in Jamaica, had similar experiences of racism whilst training in the 1960s: "They don't want a Black nurse to touch you, 'get your black hands off me'... I used to say to them, 'well Mrs so and so, you don't have a choice'."

Mavis Midgley Bryan came to Northampton from Jamaica to train as a nurse at St Andrew's Hospital in 1958. During training she was surprised as she was expected to clean the floors and windows. To Mavis's relief, as she progressed through the training she was given more responsibility and medical instruction. She lived in the nurses' accommodation with other girls from the West Indies, Spain and Ireland. In 1961, after completing training at St Andrew's, she married Ivan and went on to the Barratt Maternity Home to train in midwifery. Mavis applied for a post as a Staff Nurse at Princess Marina Hospital in 1966; she was eventually promoted to Ward Sister and continued to work at Princess Marina for twenty years until her retirement in 1986. Despite these achievements, Mavis Bryan faced barriers of discrimination whilst working for Northampton Health Authority. She applied for a Nursing Officer's post three times, only to be told that "the authorities did not want any more West Indians to be Nursing Officers."

Cynthia Awojinrin was born in Grenada and also came to Northampton to train as a nurse at St Andrew's Hospital. Arriving there in 1959, she shared Mavis Bryan's disappointment at being "made to clean the windows and scrub the floors, but hardly any care of the patients and this is my training!". She left after two years to work at St Edmund's Hospital, where she worked for two years before training as a midwife at the Barratt Maternity Home.

The nurse training of so many Caribbean settlers helped them to make a skilled contribution to many community organizations in Northamptonshire. Their general experiences of living and working in the county are described in more detail in Chapter Eight.

Community Relations Councils (CRCs) and Racial Equality Councils (WDREC, KREC, NREC)

Mike Prescod addressing WDREC

Mike Prescod trained as a social worker after military service, and soon recognized that current public services had no strategic plan to incorporate Black communities into their existing provision. In 1976 he went to work for the Northamptonshire County Council and became the first Black social worker in Northamptonshire. Taking up the fight against racism, Mike also became the first paid worker of the Wellingborough and District Community Relations Council : "the first organization that had race at the heart of its remit". With funding from Wellingborough Social Services, many Asian and Caribbean community groups soon became affiliated to the CRC. The CRC provided legal advice and general support concerning race relation issues for all individuals and organizations, both Black and White. With Home Office funding across the country, by the 1980s the CRC developed into the Wellingborough Racial Equality Council. They employed the first community relations officers, including Mike Prescod himself as a race relations and community development officer.

Pratima Dattani, a Hindu born in Uganda, arrived in Northampton in 1972. She worked for the County Council and became involved with the WDREC in 1983 as a volunteer and member, helping to develop services for the wider Black community. In the mid 1980s she became the chair of the REC, holding the position for three years: "It was a time when the organisation had very very good foundations built up from when Mike Prescod was involved and Paul (Crofts) had been there for many years." She used her different positions to complement each other: "In terms of the experience I have had both in the REC and the Black voluntary sector in Wellingborough, that's been my essential stuff in terms of building up my career." She talks of "parallel processes of a kind; having a grass roots approach to what I do in the County Council as well and looking at everything from a user perspective as opposed to just a bureaucratic kind of perspective". Between 1995 and 2002 Pratima Dattani served as chair of the Gharana Housing Association, having also been involved in establishing the Pravasi Mandal, the Asian older people's organisation.

Dipana Patel leading Diwali celebrations

Dipana Patel was also born in Uganda and arrived with her family as a child in Wellingborough in 1972. Her father was a highly respected business man and community activist back home in Africa. On arrival in Wellingborough he worked long hours in a local factory, but still found time to volunteer his services to the local Black community. Dipana herself was involved with Wellingborough Racial Equality Council from the late 1980s, through shadowing her father as he helped out at the Victoria Centre. After graduating with a Social Studies degree in 1989,

Dipana returned to Wellingborough, volunteering as a WREC committee member. Her sister Jaymini Patel helped to set up Gharana Housing and the Pravasi Mandal Asian Elderly Day Care Centre, at the same time working as a social worker for Northamptonshire Social Services with the Black elderly community. Both sisters have continuously worked between the local authority and various Black voluntary organisations over the years, identifying gaps in government service provision and working toward closing those gaps and meeting community needs, despite many setbacks and obstacles.

Anjona Roy

Anjona Roy, of Bengali Hindu descent, was born in Northampton and had an interest in politics from an early age. She attended Northampton High School where she first became involved in politics, joining the youth section of the Campaign for Nuclear Disarmament. Between 1982 and 1984 Anjona was involved in direct action at Greenham Common and in the protests against apartheid outside the South African Embassy in London. In 1993 she helped to set up the Council for Ethnic Minority Communities (CEMC), an umbrella organization supporting voluntary and community groups. In 1996 Anjona worked for Wellingborough Black Consortium (another umbrella organization), before transferring her efforts into the Northamptonshire Racial Equality Council when she was appointed as the Chief Executive of the REC in 2003. In 1997 Anjona joined the Labour Party, and in 2001 she was successful in becoming Northampton's first Black female Borough councillor.

Today the REC continues to grow and is very active, giving legal advice, support and guidance in response to complaints of racism from across Northamptonshire. It has been built on the legacy of the successful Wellingborough Community Relations Council, founded in the mid-1970s. Paul Crofts and Jenny Sebastian have played a key role in Wellingborough race relations, and have since extended local good practice further afield. Northampton and Kettering opened their own CRCs from the late 1980s onwards, aiming to support and strengthen local voluntary organisations. Today there is a unified, county-wide Northamptonshire Racial Equality Council with an organisational presence in Wellingborough, Northampton and Kettering. Its focus is upon anti-discrimination and immigration casework, but it has also continued to support various voluntary organisations. The Northamptonshire Black History Project was launched under WREC leadership in 2002, preparing the way for today's independent Northamptonshire Black History Association.

Council for Ethnic Minority Communities (CEMC)

During the 1990s Tony Michael was the driving force behind the Council for Ethnic Minority Communities, an umbrella organisation offering Black and minority ethnic community groups general advice and support. It has continued its developmental role to the present day, with founding members Tony Michael and Cliff Gulley still in post. CEMC grew out of an organisation originally called the Open Forum. June Gulley recalls that this was "where different

CEMC birthday party

statutory bodies and voluntary bodies met and discussed topical issues". The Open Forum was used to help distribute local authority funding to the appropriate voluntary or community organisations. June worked in an administrative support role, drawing upon her earlier experience with the Northampton Vietnamese Association. In 1994, after a report from Northamptonshire County Council identified several problem areas, community groups recommended setting up CEMC. An elected working group submitted a joint bid for finance, and in May 1997 CEMC was born. It became a registered charity, based first at Military Road Adult Learning Centre then at the new Northampton College building in the town centre.

Post-War Settlers from India, Pakistan and Bangladesh

Since the Second World War larger numbers of South Asian people have arrived in Northamptonshire. Britain's labour shortages in the 1950s and 1960s were met by settlers from the Indian subcontinent as well as from the Caribbean. Single men from East Pakistan (now Bangladesh) were among the early arrivals in Northamptonshire, their families often joining them many years later. People of Indian descent moved here when Idi Amin expelled Asians from Uganda in the 1970s, while many Kenyan Asians were also on the move before the restrictions on settlement imposed by the 1968 Immigration Act. The war between East and West Pakistan accelerated migration from that region before resulting in the creation of Bangladesh in 1971. During the same period there was a gradual increase in the number of settlers from India and Pakistan, including doctors and teachers as well as less highly educated workers.

People from Asia came from a range of different countries with very varied cultural and religious needs. They came from different social classes, both rich and poor, in order to escape the turmoil in their homelands. Some of their experiences are described in Chapter Nine. Like the Caribbean settlers, they suffered from the lack of specific public services designed to meet their diverse needs. Differences of language and religious custom often made the existing local services very difficult for newcomers to access.

Saeed Ahmed Pirzada, an Indian Muslim who had witnessed the partitioning of India and Pakistan in 1947, had experience of setting up voluntary public service organizations even before he arrived in Britain in 1964. Living and working in Wellingborough, he noticed how poorer families were struggling to adapt to an unfamiliar lifestyle: "you know people have large families, single earner working anti-social hours on low wages...that is a factor which is affecting their families and... when I moved to Wellingborough this was, you know, a shock to me that our families are so much struggling that they need help. And without somebody taking a lead."

Community leaders soon began to emerge, and the Asian community began to develop its own community organisations, out of a need to come together to celebrate religious and cultural festivals and to build new kinds of social cohesion. Like their Caribbean predecessors, Asian settlers identified the need to bridge the various gaps in public service provision. Voluntary organisations once again began out of the necessity for settlers to help their own community.

The Asian Advisory Panel (AAP)

One of the first organisations was the Asian Advisory Panel, set up by several business men on a voluntary basis in the mid-1970s. Sarwat Khakhar and her Muslim husband had arrived in Northamptonshire from Kenya in 1970. Her husband was instrumental in helping to establish the AAP. She remembers: "I really got involved... when Ugandans came over to this country and my husband was helping them to settle down. A lot of them were in Kettering... And there was a company that was all mainly men, who used to help them." The early arrivals needed assistance with access to housing, social security, filling in forms, advocacy and interpreting.

Wellingborough Oriental Sports and Social Club

Saeed Ahmed Pirzada was committed to improving the quality of life for his community. Like some Caribbean community leaders, he worked between the local authority and the voluntary sector: "I have been working as a social worker in addition to my job all my life." His main concern was the numbers of failing Muslim children in schools and to resolve the situation, he began teaching Bangladeshi and Pakistani children from his own home. He and his wife taught and motivated children and their families to value education. Wellingborough Oriental Sports and Social Club eventually offered cricket, football, baseball, cookery, needle work, gardening, information services and educational facilities for children and young people. More recently, Saeed has worked with the WREC and as president of the local Pakistan Welfare Association.

Wellingborough Islamic Union

Ashraf Ullah Khan has played a key role in developing support for Wellingborough Muslims. He came to Wellingborough from Pakistan in 1969 with his wife Bibi Hajara and his first son, then four months old. At that time there was no Muslim organization or mosque in Wellingborough, and only about twenty or thirty Muslim families lived in the town. In the early 1970s Ashraf Khan teamed up with Mr Din to form the Wellingborough Islamic Union. They took out a loan to purchase a house in Regent Street to be used as a mosque. However it did not have planning permission for this purpose and there were some difficulties with the Borough Council. At this moment Mr Din died and the house had to be sold to pay off the loan. However, there was sufficient money made on the sale to help purchase another house in Strode Road to be used as a mosque. This time the necessary planning permission was successfully obtained.

Islah-ul-Muslimeen

In the late 1970s the Islamic Union ceased to exist and Islah-ul-Muslimeen was formed and began to manage the mosque in Strode Road. Ashraf Khan was its first chairman, and held this position or that of general secretary until 2003. Working at the Wellingborough engineering firm Copeland and Jenkins, he also found time to become active in the Amalgamated Engineering Union and the Labour Party, as well as supporting the formation of the Wellingborough Community Relations Council in 1973 and serving on its executive committee for many years.

During the 1980s the Muslim community in Wellingborough was growing quickly. It soon numbered several hundred families, as a result of family reunions and also through inward migration from London and other parts of Britain. The Strode Road mosque was now far too small. In the mid-1980s an empty Gospel mission building at the corner of Strode Road and Winstanley Road was purchased for a new mosque, with the support of a local Bangladeshi businessman.

Islah-ul-Muslimeen links the mosque to a busy community centre which provides a wide range of community services. The Wellingborough mosque has always been for all Muslims, irrespective of their country of origin, and now has members from all over the world – Asia, the Middle East, Africa, the Caribbean, and recent converts from the local community. This is the lasting legacy of Ashraf Khan's leadership. From 1969 onwards he has steadily worked in support of the Muslim community, and of the wider community, always winning support from and working in cooperation with others.

Dostiyo

In the 1979 Kate Quazi, from South Africa, formed Dostiyo, the first Asian women and girls' group in Northampton. She was assisted by Sarwat Khakhar, Jamila Amar, Anjona Roy and Farhat Lateef.

Sarwat recalls: "Kate Quazi. She is the one who actually gave birth to this group." Farhat remembers Dostiyo originally started as an Asian women's association based in the Drapery and sharing office space with the Northampton Community Relations Council. It soon grew as more women started to seek help. Sarwat remembers the women's welfare office on Wellingborough Road; the group then moved to the Military Road Centre. Its main function was to promote friendships and well-being. The women celebrated religious and cultural

Kate Quazi with Dostiyo members

festivals, catering for a multi-national, multicultural and religious cross section of the community. Dostiyo next moved to Cloutsham Street for several years, with funding from the County Council and from the Lottery Fund, before transferring to Dunster Street where they are situated today.

Dostiyo offer support and advice services on issues of immigration, housing, benefits, education, disability support, health and social care to Asian women and girls, together with various classes and creche facilities for families. Anjona was involved in running Dostiyo during its early formation, becoming the chairperson and giving it continued support to date. In 2001 Farhat became the vice-chair of Dostiyo and in 2002 she was elected to the dual role of vice-chair and secretary. Sarwat Khakar became part of the management structure as treasurer to the group, while working part-time teaching English as a second language at the Military Road Centre, the Sikh temple and other community centres around Northamptonshire. Today Dostiyo also welcomes men, supplying separate services for them. Dostiyo now works in partnership with Social Services to deliver family support services through a seconded social worker based at the centre.

Dostiyo river trip

Muslim Women's Association of Northampton

The Muslim Women's Association started in the early 1980s. Whilst forming Dostiyo, Jamila Amar and Kate Quazi identified the need and formed a separate Muslim women's group. Its main function was to celebrate religious ceremonies. Jamila remembers: "We came to know lots of people, lots of Pakistani ladies, Bengali ladies, be it ladies from Africa, all Muslim ladies...we got them all together and they really enjoyed it." Sarwat began to work on a voluntary basis for Northamptonshire Social Services as translator in a range of languages. She also continued assisting her husband as an interpreter for women's issues: "They realized that there were certain things that women need...they wouldn't go to a man for certain problems. So that's where a couple of the ladies organized this women's welfare office on Wellingborough Road."

Jamila Amar was born in Uganda and arrived in Britain in 1972. She worked forty hours a week in a factory to help support her family, giving up her weekends and evenings to helping in various local Asian community groups. From there, Jamila became interested in doing professional care work and got a job at Quarry House as a care assistant during the 1980s, continuing her voluntary work at weekends for four years. Within the Muslim Women's Association, Jamila recalls: "We should have gone under the umbrella of Dostiyo...it was voted against...because what the group wanted Dostiyo could not provide... Because with the Islamic religion there is certain things that it does not combine... the whole group voted to go under the umbrella of Institute of Islamic Studies." Although the group separated from Dostiyo, they kept close links: "We worked together with Dostiyo, because we used to borrow Dostiyo's van and all that." Jamila continued to run the group through to the 1990s, and the organisation still survives to date.

Pravasi Mandal Asian Day Care Centre and Gharana Housing

Pravasi Mandal was established in 1984, starting out as an informal Asian community organisation for the older generation meeting at the Victoria Centre. Niranjan Jani, a Gujerati Hindu, arrived in Wellingborough in 1972. In 1995 he joined Pravasi Mandal: "It was like a friendly club with elderly people with lots of time on hand and lots of enthusiasm. They are the two things in abundance." By 1996 Niranjan was helping to formalise

Pravasi Mandal opening day

the organisation into a registered charity: "It was a landmark because without charity registration you can't do the fundraising." They gained support from the Council for Voluntary Service and Age Concern, as well from the local community: "These people have vast business experience back in East Africa. They all end up in Wellingborough and they support the project." Niranjan explains how, through firm family and community connections, many people have become successful in local business and are fulfilling their aspirations to better themselves: "That is the driving force you know for what we are today." Pravasi Mandal began to take the lead in the provision of elderly day care services, obtaining support and funding from Northamptonshire Social Services and Northampton Health Authority. In August 2002 the Day Care Centre was officially opened, and by 2003 it had over four hundred members.

Jamila Amar began working for Gharana Housing as a Meals on Wheels supervisor in 1999: "I was managing seven staff there and I did very well, and then the position came up for a community care officer. And I applied for it, I got the job." She was based in Wellingborough at the head office, where Gharana have another sheltered housing scheme for more frail and dependent residents. She also became warden for Nazarana, sheltered accommodation for the elderly in Northampton for more independent residents: "Nazarana is managed by Gharana Housing Association and Nazarana is property for East Midlands Housing Association...it's not for Asians only, but we've got the Asians only. It was a multicultural organization but the people who applied here who were not Asian did not accept it, because majority were Asians."

The Wellingborough Hindu Association and the Hindu Community Centre

Shashi Dholakia, an Indian from Kenya, arrived in Wellingborough in 1966. Like so many activists, he was already heavily involved in supporting and organising his community back home before coming to England. As a young man he joined the Wellingborough Hindu Association and was involved in helping to set up the Hindu temple in Highfield Road. After acquiring a base, he began by establishing "a sports club, the youth wing of the Hindu Association." The Hindu community was small at the time, but there were over a thousand users by the early 1990s. A new, purpose-built community centre was urgently required as people came from around Northamptonshire and from up and down Britain for religious festivals. Funding to purchase a new building came from the Wellingborough Hindu community in the early 1980s, and from 1993 he became chairman for the Hindu Association as well as a councillor for Castle Ward, Wellingborough.

Shashi Dholakia

In 2002 Shashi Dholakia was invited to India by the Indian High Commission to receive the Presidential Award called Hind Rutten, which means "Jewel of India". This honour was granted for his life-long commitment to helping his community: "It was like winning a Eurovision Song Contest for the United Kingdom and, you know, I was touched because I thought not only did I carry my Hindu brothers and sisters from Wellingborough, Northamptonshire, but I thought I took United Kingdom with me to receive that award."

Vishwa Hindu Parishad (VHP)

Bhikubhai Dudhia, a Gujerat Hindu, arrived in the UK in 1971. Now retired, he used to be a teacher and worked in Northampton teaching Gujerati to children. He helped to support the local Hindu organizations as a committee member for over twelve years: "In Northampton there are two or three Hindu organizations but the main one is VHP, Vishwa Hindu Parishad. It is the umbrella organisation which embraces all the organizations and it conducts all the community activities". VHP is funded by the local Hindu community's contributions; its functions include the celebration of religious and cultural festivals, and it is also linked to Hindu politics in India. More recently Bhikubhai Dudhia has helped to support Nazarana: "contacting people, getting contacts and getting their views, how they are living there and talk to them about their life and experiences". Nazarana was set up in the 1990s and it "caters for elderly people, it's elderly people's home and it's giving facilities to the older generation which they cannot find in their homes".

During the 1980s Jamila Amar became an active member of Vishwa Hindu Parishad, though herself a Muslim. She explains that she learnt a lot from its treasurer and president: both gentlemen were good friends and advisers who showed her how to run an organisation. However, "I resigned ...when that... (Ayodha) mosque was destroyed in India. And every time we sat in the meeting they just could not speak about it, because I was the only Muslim sitting amongst them... I (also) resigned because I had too much by then, because I was running Muslim Women Association."

Northampton Indian Hindu Welfare Organisation (IHWO)

In 1996 Neelam Aggarwal, Ash Bedi and Ashok Kapoor founded the Indian Hindu Welfare Organisation. Neelam recalls that the group arose to "engage and enrich the lives of all Hindus, meeting their social, educational, religious and welfare needs". IHWO works in partnership with other community and statutory organisations, such as the Sikh community and the County and Borough Councils, for example in connection with the popular annual Diwali celebrations in Northampton which bring about community cohesion between different religious and cultural groups. In 2004 Neelam helped to create Northampton Utsav Organisation, a group that aims to brings different cultural groups together to celebrate various cultural and religious festivals. They have taken the lead in the Diwali lights celebration in the town centre of Northampton since their formation.

Neelam Aggarwal

Neelam arrived in Northampton in 1981. By 1991 she had joined Dostiyo, becoming part of the Management Committee then later vice chair. During the early 1990s she also joined NREC, again becoming part of the management committee and vice chair. At the same time she started working at the Multicultural Resources Centre, funded through Section 11 and the County Council, until funding came to an end in 1994. In 1997 Neelam became a non-executive Director of the Northamptonshire Mental Health Trust, then later of Northampton Primary Care Trust. She also co-ordinated a government-funded project involving families in schools, working with the County Council and the Council for Ethnic Minority Communities. More recently, in July 2007 the BME Sub Regional Thematic Partnership was launched under Neelam's chairmanship, bringing together a wide range of Black organisations and linking them to the County Council. Today the IHWO continues to flourish, as part of a growing network of voluntary organisations. It is campaigning to raise support and finance for the Northampton Kutumbh Centre. This "extended family" centre, proposed for Lings Way, Lumbertubs, will meet a wide range of religious, social and educational needs.

Patel Samaj of Northampton

Patel Samaj of Northampton is a Hindu charity organisation that was formed in 1998; they are affiliated to the Hindu Forum of Britain. The main instigators behind the group are Suresh Patel, the President, Surendra Patel, Suresh B Patel, J V Patel, Mukesh Patel, Vipin Patel and J S Patel. Suresh explains: "We are still serving the community from various premises, we don't have our own. We have over two thousand members. Last five years under my chairmanship we have really grown." Fund raising is a major part of the group's cause, for example helping to raise money for floods and famine relief in India in 2000 and 2005. Patel Samaj runs a weekly youth club, Bollywood dance classes, a walking club, a men's business and social club, a ladies' club, a club for the elderly, family gatherings, and various cultural and religious activities. The group still continues to grow in strength today, and often invites the wider Northampton community to participate in its festivals.

Patel Samaj Irish dance class

Northampton Bangladeshi Association (NBA)

The Northampton Bangladeshi Association was born out of Al-Jamat, an informal Bengali Muslim group that would meet to celebrate religious and cultural festivals. Akram Zaman was one of its first leaders and continues his role today. He contributed to the

Asian Advisory Panel and the Race Forum in the late 1970s. He has also been active in politics and has helped to develop and encourage others into politics, including Yousuf Miah.

Yousef Miah was born in Bangladesh in 1976, and brought up in Northampton. His father was involved in helping to set up support and social events for the Bangladeshi community through the local mosque. Yousef remembers: "Back in the 80s the Bangladeshi community used to be in the same place as the mosque: the mosque was predominantly a male-dominated place." The young Yousuf accompanied his father during his many hours of voluntary work. He followed that example after university, when young Bangladeshi people in Northampton "realised that things weren't as they should be so we thought about maybe separating the social and religious aspects of the community; working with various government departments and everybody else created the Northampton Bangladeshi Association." The NBA moved to an old school building on the Barrack Road for four years, until they opened their own brand-new, purpose-built building. The NBA is funded by contributions from

Yousuf Miah

the Bangladeshi community, local businesses, local government grants and charitable funds. Yousuf became managing director of the NBA, seeing it through its transition to the new premises. Today it is run by the centre manager, Abdul Latif. The NBA is concerned with the welfare of the community, providing for educational, recreational and social needs. Yousuf Miah became one of the first Black Conservative councillors in Northamptonshire, and has ambitions to enter Parliament.

Meanwhile Bangladeshi women are also organizing themselves. Sophia and Rufia Miah were born and grew up in Northampton. Rufia, currently studying for a degree in social work, previously worked across

NBA women's group at their allotment

voluntary and statutory services, from Dostiyo and NBA to the Camrose Centre. Today Sophia also works between local government services, at the NBA and Camrose Centre Sure Start for Children and Families and Earl Spencer Primary School. She states: "My aim is to turn these women around, Bangladeshi women to actually stand up for their rights."

Today the NBA has become the central point for the Bengali community's social, health and welfare needs. At the same time its premises are becoming a facility for the wider, culturally mixed, local community.

Islamic Pakistani Community Centre (IPCC)

Farhat Lateef was born in Lahore. A Pakistani Muslim, she arrived in Britain in 1974. Both Farhat and her husband have played an important part in developing the Northampton Islamic Pakistani Community Centre. The IPCC was started by Farhat Lateef's husband and several of his friends from the community during the 1980s. They founded their organisation in Colwyn Road, Northampton. Farhat has been working for many years as a teaching assistant at the Military Road Primary School, now Castle Primary School. When the centre was first set up a number of local residents petitioned against its opening. Farhat comments: "and now just think about it, I'm in that school and those residents, they all come there with their children!" The centre became well-established, serving all ages and both genders though men's and women's activities were separated for religious reasons. Social and recreational facilities were provided, including a meal service for the elderly, trips out, prayers and religious or festive celebrations.

Northampton Sikh Community Centre and Youth Club (SCCYC) and Kettering Sikh Temple

The Northampton Sikh Community Centre was formed in October 1996. Its aim is to "provide services that other organisations could not provide to Sikhs; SCCYC exists to meet the social, cultural and educational needs of the community by involving community members in shaping their own lives". The Centre is a registered charity. Based in St Georges Street, Northampton, it is sponsored by the County and Borough Councils and various other funding bodies. It has facilities that provide a whole range of community activities, including a gymnasium, work shops, computer classes and a Punjabi School. Services are offered to Sikhs of all ages, including issue-based activities related to health and integration, as well as many educational and cultural events.

Meharban and Mohinder Kaur Plahay, members of the Kettering Sikh community, were both born in the 1930s. Mr Plahay is from Kenya and Mrs Plahay from Tanzania, and they arrived in Northampton in the late 1960s. Interviewed by the Northamptonshire Black History Project in 2002, they talked about the lack of services to support new arrivals in those early days: "Deported from Uganda, we were in Corby then they came just in the clothes. In the clothes they were wearing." The couple described helping new arrivals to get access to food, clothing and accommodation: "I used to go with the Mrs Dear, Doctor's wife, and we used to go and get money from the Social Services; I used to go with her to get some grocery, Indian grocery." Nowadays the Sikhs in Kettering are well-supported through their own local temple and its various community services.

Conclusion

The men and women who have done such important work in providing public services in Northamptonshire have almost always started out from grassroots community organisations. Whether in education, health or social welfare, they have helped improve their own lives by helping others. After getting their foot in the door and earning themselves respect as voluntary providers of public services, they have been able to influence local and national policy, to insist upon equal opportunities, and gradually to contribute towards social inclusion within Northamptonshire and wider British society.

The growth of local community organizations is a complicated story, and one which never stands still. In the first decade of the twenty-first century, established Black and Asian communities in Northamptonshire have been joined by many newcomers from different parts of the world. New organisations continue to emerge. Northampton's large Somali community, for example, has recently founded its own organisations, including the Somali Forum, the Women and Girls'

Northampton's Mayor meets the Somali community

Group, the Youth Council, the Northamptonshire Somali Community and the Somali Health Forum. A Northamptonshire Muslim Council has been established, and there are plans to expand both Muslim and Hindu places of worship in the next few years. Meanwhile evangelical Christian churches continue to multiply under the leadership of Black British, African and Caribbean pastors, providing social as well as religious support to their congregations. Settlers have chosen to support each other in many different ways over the years, and it seems likely that the next generation of newcomers will continue to expand Northamptonshire's strong traditions of voluntary community service.

Further Reading and Primary Sources:

Thanks are due to all those whose recorded life histories have been deposited in the NBHP oral history archive at the Northamptonshire Record Office, and to others who have given oral testimony. Community archives containing documents and pictures have also been deposited at the Northamptonshire Record Office, including records of the United Social Club, West Indian Parents' Association, Sankofa and Dostiyo.

The Northamptonshire Black History Association database contains references for many individuals and organisations: www.northants-black-history.org.uk

Local newspapers, including the *Northampton Chronicle and Echo*, are another important source of evidence.

See also:
ACES, *Cold Arrival: Life in a Second Homeland* (Northampton: ACES, 1998)
P. Gilroy, *There Ain't No Black in the Union Jack* (London: Routledge, 1987)

This chapter was written by Donna Palmer-Smith

Conclusion

Our book has presented you with a historical portrait of Northamptonshire's links to the wider world, and especially to the former British Empire. A long and varied history has been brought to life by stories of individual human achievement, whether in the recent past or hundreds of years ago.

Some people say the twenty-first century is a "post-colonial" era. We are now living in a world which is no longer dominated by European colonial rule over large areas of Asia, Africa and the Caribbean. But no-one should deny the role of empires, and especially the British Empire, in our shared past. Neither should the history of colonisation obscure the longer-term histories of Africa and Asia, which reveal the British Isles as comparatively backward and unimportant during most of human history.

The research and educational work of the Northamptonshire Black History Association leads us to conclude that sharing the past contributes towards shaping a well-informed and well-integrated future for Northamptonshire and the rest of Britain. Our research into the Black and Asian presence in this county is being gradually replicated elsewhere. Local histories of global travel and settlement offer fresh perspectives on Britain's role in the world. They also provide amazing stories of human endurance and human creativity. The experiences of all the people included in this book have helped to make Northamptonshire the diverse and interesting place it is today.

A lot of local people worked together to create this book. Some helped to put the past half-century on the record through their life story interviews. Others lent documents and photographs, or undertook the patient work of trawling the archives for historical evidence from earlier times.

Northamptonshire Black History Association thanks everyone who has contributed, in whatever way. We also hope that many readers will want to add to the history offered here. Your help is needed to continue the work of discovering and understanding Northamptonshire's local history in its global context.

Finding out More

The final section of this book is a short do-it-yourself guide to Northamptonshire Black History. If you have enjoyed the story so far, why not make your own contribution to finding out more? Here are some places to start.

Northamptonshire Black History Association

Northamptonshire Black History Association is a voluntary organisation which undertakes research and educational activities linked to local Black and Asian History. Formed in 2005, it has built on the legacy of the lottery-funded Northamptonshire Black History Project (2002-05) and upon earlier research by groups and individuals. NBHA has close links to local Black communities, and also works in partnership with local agencies responsible for education and the preservation of historical records.

The NBHA website gives you an idea of the range of our work: www.northants-black-history.org.uk. Our searchable database presents detailed references to most of the local sources for this book. Our oral history archive at the Northamptonshire Record Office is the outcome of many years' work. It is a fitting monument to the first post-war generation of settlers in Northamptonshire and a treasury of wonderful stories, as well as a valuable source for future historians.

We have achieved funding for a number of educational projects, large and small, from sponsors including the University of Northampton and Northamptonshire County Council, as well as the Heritage Lottery Fund. In the future our work will include new project work and new research, as well as the promotion and custodianship of work completed to date.

The outcomes of our work so far include performances, films and school curriculum materials as well as books, exhibitions and a quarterly Newsletter. Membership activities are very varied, including day trips to places of historical interest as well as talks, theatre visits, and many different kinds of research. This book has been authored and edited by NBHA members. NBHA also runs courses in Black History in partnership with the University of Northampton.

We invite all our supporters to join NBHA for a small annual fee, and to take an active part in deciding the way ahead for Northamptonshire Black History.

Contact details:

Northamptonshire Black History Association
Doddridge Centre
109 St James Road
Northampton NN5 5LD

Email: admin@northants-black-history.org.uk
Phone: 01604 590967

NBHA visits the Equiano exhibition

Black History in Northamptonshire Schools

The Northamptonshire Black History Association is helping teachers and pupils to fulfil National Curriculum requirements and government recommendations related to the teaching of British History.

The case for teaching Black History relates to general educational needs as well as to the need to provide all pupils with a meaningful map of the past.

The Ajegbo Report of 2007 argued that schools need a curriculum which "addresses issues of ethnicity, culture, language and religion and the multiple identities children inhabit. It is education for mutual understanding and respect which gives pupils a real understanding of who lives in the UK today, of why we are here, and of what they as pupils can contribute" (*Curriculum Review: Diversity and Citizenship*, DFES, 2007, p.15).Recent revisions to the National Curriculum are closely linked to this report, and to the government's concern to promote stronger social cohesion. The 2008

Nikki Taylor at Eastfield Primary School, Northampton

Secondary History Curriculum makes specific reference to the histories of diversity, migration and settlement, slavery and empire. We hope that revisions to the Primary Curriculum following from the Rose Review (2007-08) will also promote an inclusive approach to our shared past. The current Key Stage 1 school curriculum focuses on local and family histories, as well as on learning about people from around the world. At Key Stage 2, children are required to learn about British, European and World dimensions of the past, and to develop an understanding of ethnic and cultural diversity.

In response to the evolving school curriculum, NBHA has published a series of curriculum packs which make it possible for every teacher and every school to teach relevant aspects of Black History at appropriate levels. *Walter Tull: Sport, War and Challenging Adversity* is available in different versions for KS1, KS2 and KS3. All Northamptonshire schools have received free hard copies of these packs, which also include electronic resources. The packs explore the life of Cobblers footballer and British Army officer Walter Tull. *From Slavery to Emancipation* is available free of charge on the NBHA website, providing a local dimension to a major aspect of the KS3 History curriculum. This pack also looks at aspects of African history prior to the Transatlantic Slave Trade, and at the role of free and enslaved Africans in the Abolition movement. *Representations of Empire: Learning from Objects* is designed for KS2 and KS3 pupils. It uses museum-related and object-based activities to provide insights into the lives and perspectives of different peoples within the former British Empire. Northamptonshire Museums Service has collaborated with NBHA to produce three loan boxes of original artefacts to accompany the hard-copy pack. Together these resources provide good cross-cultural themes and links through topics such as missionaries, the Opium Wars, Benin, slavery (including authentic slave implements), the Scramble for Africa, trade and tourism, craft and collectors. *Living Memories* draws on the vast oral history archive at the Northamptonshire Record Office. The experiences of people from local Black and Asian communities can be used to enhance recent History and Citizenship topics at KS2 and KS3, as well as for delivering the English and ICT curriculum. The pack includes recorded interview extracts and is available in hard copy. *Northamptonshire in Global Context* consists of a series of mini-resource packs, designed by teachers and accompanied by activities and suggestions for mainstreaming them into the National Curriculum. These resources are available on the NBHA website, and are supported by the present book. The book which you are reading, *Sharing the Past: Northamptonshire Black History*, offers teachers straightforward access to the basic knowledge needed in order to teach Black British History from a local perspective. We have aimed to provide a long-term overview of Northamptonshire's diverse history.

Contact details:

Full information on all the NBHA curriculum packs is available from our website: www.northants-black-history.org.uk

Hard copies of three curriculum packs are available at £20/£25 plus postage from Northamptonshire Black History Association, Doddridge Centre, 109 St James Road, Northampton NN5 5LD (01604 590967):
Walter Tull: Sport, War and Challenging Adversity,
Representations of Empire: Learning from Objects
Living Memories

Free electronic copies of two curriculum packs are available from the NBHA website: www.northants-black-history.org.uk:
From Slavery to Emancipation
Northamptonshire in Global Context

NBHA's general history of the Black and Asian presence in Northamptonshire is on sale from the Doddridge Centre and from local booksellers:
Sharing the Past: Northamptonshire Black History (Northampton: NBHA, 2008)

Black History Resources at the Northamptonshire Record Office

The Record Office is the place of deposit for much of the written heritage of Northamptonshire and holds material from the twelfth century to the present day. The archives are created by a wide range of organisations, families and estates, parish churches, businesses, societies and individuals. The records relate primarily to the county of Northamptonshire. However, the records of the diocese of Peterborough (covering Northamptonshire, the Soke of Peterborough and Rutland) and some records relating to other counties are also held.

Any records might contain references to the Black presence in the county and the Northamptonshire Black History Project 2002-2005 extracted many of these from a variety of sources. The main sources are likely to be parish or church registers (recording baptisms, marriages and burials), census returns, wills, school and legal records. In addition, the county is particularly rich in the records of landed families who often employed black servants or had interests abroad. These would be useful places to search for references to Black History, although they are by no means the only records available.

Searching for evidence of the Black presence in historical sources can be time-consuming and frustrating! Reading old handwriting can also be a challenge. There is obviously no guarantee of success: a particular bundle of correspondence might prove to be very useful or contain no information at all. We recommend that the Northamptonshire Black History Association database is used as a first resort. This is likely to pinpoint known information about black families or individuals living in particular places and act as a platform upon which to base further research.

In addition to the general sources, the Record Office holds specific information about Black History in Northamptonshire. The Northamptonshire Black History Project co-ordinated and processed over two hundred interviews with members of Black communities in the county. The interviews are made available on tape with a summary of the contents and a full transcript of the interview. These form a unique record of peoples' experiences and feelings on a variety of different subjects from first arriving in Britain to employment, housing, food, relationships and of course, the weather!

Ghana Union records deposited at the Record Office

In addition, some Black community and voluntary groups have chosen to deposit their records in the Record Office. These are a valuable addition to our holdings as they help to give a full picture of the diverse communities in the county. The records include Racial Equality Council for Wellingborough and Northampton, Liberian Association, Somali Association, Ghana Union, Dostiyo Asian Women and Girls Group, Northampton Afro-Caribbean Association (NACO), United Social Club (Afro-Caribbean), West Indian Parents Association (WIPA), Sankofa – black mental health charity. These records are generally available for consultation, although some more modern material may be subject to the provisions of the Data Protection Act and not produced to researchers without permission from the depositor.

The collections held by the Record Office are being added to all the time and this introduction can only scratch the surface of the amount and type of material available. The Record Office is always keen to receive new information and material relating to the diverse history of Northamptonshire.

Contact details:

Northamptonshire Record Office
Wootton Hall Park
Northampton NN4 8BQ

Email: archivist@northamptonshire.gov.uk
Phone: 01604 762129

Northamptonshire Studies Collection

Located in Northamptonshire Central Library, the Northamptonshire Studies Collection contains printed material, such as books, pamphlets, periodicals, newspapers and maps dating from the late sixteenth century to the present. There are also around a hundred thousand photographic images and eight thousand prints and engravings. Original manuscripts can also be viewed, notably the John Clare, Sir Henry Dryden and Charles Bradlaugh MP collections, and the minutes of the Kettering Anti-Slavery Auxiliary Association (1831-35).

The earliest Black presence is commonly found in parish registers, dating back to the mid-sixteenth century. Copies are available on microfiche. They are supplemented by name indexes to some registers and monumental inscriptions for churches and graveyards. Personal information is also contained in census returns from 1841 – 1901, covering every household in England and Wales, with details of people's age, occupation and place of birth, though not ethnicity. The returns for Northamptonshire are available on microfiche and microfilm, while an online service enables the researcher to call on censuses beyond the county.

The most abundant source for Black History is local newspapers, dating from 1720 (*Northampton Mercury*) to present. They are held on microfilm and it is useful to note that some newspapers, for example, the *Kettering Leader, Rushden Echo and Argus*, and the *Wellingborough Journal*, are held in the relevant local library. Earlier newspapers concentrated on national and international events and show how local people interacted with these. Items range from small notices for the sale of slaves and reports of notable Black visitors to the county, to debates on the abolition of slavery and other political causes. During the nineteenth century the newspapers start to reflect ordinary life, covering poverty and crime, social events, sport and leisure. Here you will find notices and reviews of Black entertainers, achievements of Black sportsmen, visiting politicians and the misdeeds of local felons. The *Northampton Independent* is especially useful for social activities during the twentieth century. A collection of newscuttings (c.1720- 1930) arranged by place and subject is held in a closed-access area, so you will need to ask library staff to get them for you. Other newscuttings date from c.1970 and record the more recent histories of local Black communities.

Further references are found in the ephemera collection, that is, material originally designed for a short life span, such as posters, programmes, invitations and notices. Several

NBHP receives a national libraries' award, 2005

boxes of political handbills and posters highlight the anti-slavery debate, while two boxes of playbills provide links to Black entertainers. Images of Black entertainers, notable visitors and residents, are held within the photograph collection dating back to c.1870. Photographs of early portraits of Black people are also located here.

Transcripts of documents held by the National Archives, from medieval times to the eighteenth century, are available in a collection of volumes. Of note are those relating to the Commissioners for Plantations, America and West Indies. The Northampton Record Society volumes also include transcripts of documents, ranging from medieval records to militia lists.

Biographies and histories of local families help uncover Black slaves and servants, while parish histories and newsletters chronicle notable Black residents. A variety of subjects are covered within the whole collection. For example, a history of the Northamptonshire Regiment or a sale catalogue for the contents of large country house will uncover the county's links to the old British Empire and the world, while broader studies of crime, education and the health service will provide a context for your studies, as will sources such as maps and trade directories.

The Northamptonshire Studies Collection, therefore, provides an important resource for research into Northamptonshire Black History. Visitors will find extracts containing references to the Black presence in the county have been collected together in several file boxes and these provide a good starting point for new researchers.

Contact details:

Northamptonshire Studies Librarian
Northamptonshire Central Library
Abington Street
Northampton
NN1 2BA

Email: enquiredirect@northamptonshire.gov.uk
Phone: 01604 462040

Northampton Museums Service

Northampton Museums Service forms part of Northampton Borough Council and includes two museum sites: Northampton Museum and Art Gallery on Guildhall Road and Abington Museum, which is a Grade 1 listed building located within Abington Park.

Northampton Museums Service's mission is to provide an accessible and welcoming learning environment where the people of Northampton, the county and beyond can be engaged, inspired and challenged through the museum sites and their collections. Northampton Museums aim to provide accessible and diverse opportunities for all people to learn about Northampton, its people and its past.

There are many collections held by the Museum that have meaningful connections to Black History. The Museum owns a pair of gold metal-thread stockings said to belong to Josephine Baker during her time as a singer and dancer at the Folies Bergères in Paris. Made famous by her banana dance, Josephine also went on to serve with the French Resistance during the Second World War. The stockings were made during the 1930s and as a result of the metal thread, could only be worn for five minutes' dancing as they took the skin off feet!

However, the majority of items related to Black History form part of the ethnography collection. The ethnographic material held at Northampton Museum was acquired by the museum mainly by donation between the late nineteenth century and the late twentieth century. The objects come from a wide geographical spread – Asia, Oceania, Australia, Africa, North and South America and a few pieces from distinct ethnic groups within Europe. The larger part of the collection comes from Africa. The diversity of these objects is a positive aspect of this collection, providing excellent opportunities to explore cross-cultural themes.

Exploring Northampton Museum's ethnographic collection

Northampton Museums Service is delighted to have worked in partnership with Northamptonshire Black History Association on the Shaping the Future education project, which aimed to provide greater educational access to the museum's diverse ethnography collection. The end result has been the creation of a resource pack targeting Key Stages 2 and 3, with a special emphasis on History and Geography. Three ethnography loan boxes, containing ethnographic artefacts from the museums' collections, have complemented the resource pack. The loan boxes are available to schools from Northampton Museum's education department.

The Museum has also worked in partnership with Northamptonshire Black History Association on the recent 'Hands on History' project. Local artist Daxa Parmar was commissioned to create a resource using oral histories collected by NBHA, focusing on the subject of six peoples' experiences of moving from their countries of origin to Northamptonshire. The resource takes the form of a decorated globe that opens into segments, with each segment representing a person's life. When opened up, the globe plays six different oral histories relating to people from Liberia, Kenya, Japan, Korea, Montserrat and Bangladesh. The resource reflects the cultural diversity of Northamptonshire, and is also available for loan from Northampton Museum and Art Gallery.

The ethnographic collections can be viewed at the museum storage facility on request, and all enquiries are welcomed.

Contact details:

Northampton Museums Service
Northampton Museum and Art Gallery
Guildhall Road
Northampton NN1 1DP

Email: museums@northampton.gov.uk
Phone: 01604 838111

People

Northamptonshire Places

Note: Northampton and Northamptonshire occur throughout and have not been indexed.

Places Outside Northamptonshire

Note: Africa, India and the Caribbean (West Indies) occur throughout and have not been indexed. See the Contents list at the front of the book for place-related chapter titles.

Topics and Organisations